STAGEPLAYS.COM

How to Survive a Zombie Apocalypse
&
How to Survive a Zombie Apocalypse Re-loaded

Two One-act Plays

First performed Edinburgh Fringe 2010 with the following cast:

Ben Muir
Jess Napthine
David Ash
Lee Cooper

PERFORMANCE RIGHTS

Opening intro music is available from Funcast Ltd

Each of the segments of the show are individually titled and can be performed as sketches

Characters

Although the 4 characters from the original show have been portrayed as both male or female, you may present the seminar in any gender mix you wish

If so, some aspects of the seminar script will need altering in order to present characters as alternate genders and should any lines need to be changed, please contact the author for approval (pronoun changes do not require approval)

The Original Characters were ...

Dr Dale Seslick
The Seminar leader. Cool, Calm, Collected, Charismatic. Fluent in zombie survival lore, he is never stumped for an answer. He punctuates his training seminars with continual use of hand gestures and buzz words

Judy O'Dea
Dr Dale's second in command. She is scientific to a fault. Smart and to the point. She is the one who attempts to control the other two members of the team, although often gets drawn into the insanity unwillingly, she continues to act and react as if everything was carrying on normally

Donald Straite
The aged survivalist who has followed every conspiracy theory in the book and has attempted and succeeded many difficult training exercises (he once lived for seven days up a flag pole with nothing to eat but a cheese sandwich) Very keen to be involved in all aspects of training but can get easily distracted if there is a pretty lady in the audience

Tristen Granger
Dr Dale's nephew. He tries so, so hard but has absolutely no idea what is going on during the seminar. His stupidity is that of a childish wonderment - and he always tries to listen and understand what's going on... until his mind drifts and he starts thinking about puppies and clouds

As the audience enters the auditorium, they are greeted by Donald, Judy and Tristen who supply each of them with sticky badges that they can write their names on.

Inside, the stage is set with a lectern centre and four chairs - two either side and slightly back from the lectern.

Once the audience are in, the cast leaves and the lights dim. The opening track begins and Judy, Donald and Tristen re-enter at the specific points in the music that reference their area of expertise. They sit on the chairs Donald Far SR, Judy Near SR, Tristen far SL.

At the end of the music Dr Dale enters and stands behind the lectern

DALE: Good evening and welcome to How To Survive a Zombie Apocalypse, I'm Dr Dale, author of Dr Dale's Zombie Dictionary and founder of the School of Survival or as we like to call it S.O.S (*hand gesture*) and I'm here to teach you today - How To Survive A Zombie Apocalypse. Now here at the School of Survival... or S.O.S. (*hand gesture*) we don't believe in just standing there and talking at you (*hand gesture*), expecting you to soak it all up like a sponge. No. That's not how we roll. (*hand gesture*) No - we believe in Inclusion with a capital I. (*hand gesture*) Working together as a team. Inviting you to participate. Invoking Team Work And Togetherness. (*hand gesture*). We expect you to get involved with us. Share your thoughts, theories and ideas. In fact, to start you off slowly, let's just try a little bit of that inclusion now. Very simple question for you. I want to know, how many people here believe that as of this moment that they could survive a zombie apocalypse.

Audience put hands up. Dr Dale reacts accordingly with surprise or disappointment.

DALE: Okay, well let's break it down shall we, let's put this in levels. Let's see what varying degrees of survival expertise we have here. Now put your hands up if you truly believe you could survive. Now when I say truly believe I mean you know where you'd go, you know what weapons you'd use, you know which family member you'd kill.

Audience put hands up. Dale reacts accordingly.

DALE: Okay, now who thinks they are at an intermediate level? You've got a good chance of survival. You've seen some zombie films, played zombie games, read zombie books. You've got a basic idea about the zombie mythology.

Audience puts hands up and Dale reacts

DALE: Okay, now who here couldn't care less about the zombie apocalypse and has been dragged along here by someone else against their will?

Audience puts hands up - usually it requires encouragement from Dale to keep their hands up

DALE: Okay, that's good, no, be honest, keep your hands up, we need to see what levels we're dealing with here today, nobody's going to make fun of you. (*Pauses*) Okay. Stand up! Now don't be alarmed, we're not here to embarrass you, everyone just turn and look at this person. Look at them closely. Stare at them. You see this person here shouldn't be mocked for coming here with no natural awareness of the fact that they would die the moment the apocalypse began. Now, this person should be applauded. Applauded for not only their honesty, but realising that they had a problem and acting on it. Acting on the fact they know nothing and coming here to join us to learn and ultimately thrive and survive when the dead revive. So, give them a round of applause.

As the applause begins Tristen stands up and starts singing

TRISTEN: You're special! You're special! You're a very special girl! You're Special! You're a very Special girl!

DALE: Tristen…. Tristen! What did we say about the special song? We said we wouldn't sing it anymore didn't we…. It can mean other things.

Tristen sits slightly confused but in agreement

DALE: Okay, now we know a little bit about you. That we've got some experts and remedials. I think maybe it's time I introduced you to some special people who will be working closely with me to work closely with you. You see no man works alone on such a great endeavour as learning how to survive. No, I work alone as a team, and I'd like to introduce you to that team now. First off, our survival expert Mr Donald Straite.

Donald stands and steps forward

DONALD: Hello, I'm Donald Straite, and I'm a survival expert. Do you know. I once survived for a week on just a cheese sandwich. A week. Yes.

DALE: Thank you, Donald.

Donald sits

DALE: Donald is our survival expert, an expert indeed, as you can see, so far he has survived a very, very long time. Next up is my science expert, Judy O'Dea.
Judy stands up and steps forward

JUDY: Hello, I'm Judy O'Dea and I do experiments and things.

Judy sits down

DALE: Okay, thank you Judy, and finally. Tristen.

Tristen stands up

TRISTEN: Hello! I'm Tristen. Judy does experiments on me.

Tristen sits

DALE: Now, of course, we don't just experiment on Tristen at the School of Survival. Obviously, the very nature of learning how to survive a zombie apocalypse is that there hasn't been one yet, so no actual zombies exist at the moment so we have to do a lot of theorising, experimentation and looking on Wikipedia. As there are no live (or dead) zombie specimens around we do do some experimentation on Tristen, but nothing too dangerous… we do those kinds of experiments on the homeless. No, it's fine. Completely fine. Nobody notices when they go missing and they'll do anything for a sandwich. Now - we've all met each other, we all know what we're here for, I think that the first thing to do is discover all about what a zombie is.

WHAT IS A ZOMBIE?(*The heading to this segment of the play might be displayed on an overhead projector or flip chart*)

Dale remains at the lectern.
The team get into position - Donald stands POSITION A far SR to Dale at the front of the stage (preferably near a female audience member of a legal age). Judy stands POSITION B far SL at the front of the stage. And Tristen sits POSITION C in the front row of the audience directly in front of Dr Dale (or several rows back if there is a centre aisle)

DALE: You see, if you've done any research into zombies, you'll know that there are several different forms a zombie could take. There's parasitic, viral, genetic, supernatural, dead, undead…. But here at the School of Survival we deal with only one specific kind of zombie so we know where to focus our research and keep the variables at a minimum, and that particular zombie has four rules attached to it that we're going to go through now. If you're planning to make notes then now might be a good time to start…. Okay! Rule Number One : A Zombie is -

Dale points to Donald

DONALD: Dead!

DALE: A zombie is…

Dale points to Donald

DONALD: Dead.

DALE: Thank you Donald. Yes, a zombie is dead! In some forms of media such as 28 days later, 28 weeks later, Left 4 Dead Zombies are portrayed as live human beings that have been infected by some form of virus that makes them crave human flesh or a little bit angry. These are not zombies. A live human being who wants to eat another live human being is called a cannibal and this is not 'How To Survive A Cannibal Apocalypse' that's next year. So! Rule number one. A zombie is...

Dale points at Donald

DONALD: Dead!

DALE: Excellent! Rule number two concerns how one becomes a zombie. Now in the cases of other zombies it could be because of a virus, it could be radioactive gas, it could be magic space dust or a parasite could attach itself to your head like a jaunty hat. But in the case of our zombie. The infection is passed on by...

Dale points at Judy

JUDY: Biting!

DALE: Which means if you are...

Dale points at Judy

JUDY: Bitten

DALE: By a zombie you will end up...

Dale points at Donald

DONALD: Dead.

DALE: Very good. So next up we're going to learn how to kill a zombie. Well, we know that we can't technically kill a zombie because it is already...

Dale points at Donald

DONALD: Dead.

DALE: But we can stop it in its tracks. Stop it being a threat. Annihilate it and we do this by destroying the...

Dale points at Tristen. Donald also mouths the answer to a female audience member sat near him.

TRISTEN: Brain.

DALE: Yes we must...

TRISTEN: Dr Dale! Dr Dale!

DALE: What?

TRISTEN: Donald said it too. I thought Brain was supposed to be mine.

DALE: Did you Donald?

DONALD: Well, yes, I was just helping Tristen out.

TRISTEN: I don't need your help! Brain is mine. Tell him, Dr Dale.

DALE: Donald, we did say that we'd let Tristen have a go this evening didn't we.

DONALD: Yes, I suppose.

DALE: Right, we'll try it again. You must destroy the...

TRISTEN: Brain!

Donald mouths it to the woman again

TRISTEN: He did it again!

DALE: Right, Donald. I know exactly what this is. That lady is obviously trying to distract you. She's been flirting since you sat down, Donald.

DONALD: Well, I...

DALE: That's no excuse, though. Donald, we talked about this earlier. Tristen is the brains and you're dead.

DONALD: Yes, I know, but...

DALE: No buts, I want you to move away from her. I will have no distraction in my seminars. Donald, go and stand over there (*Points to position B*) Judy you come over here and keep an eye on her (Points to *Position A*) and if there's any more trouble from her you know what to do.

JUDY: Oh yes, Dr Dale.

Judy and Donald swap places so Donald is now at B and Judy is at A

DALE: Okay, right, well, I think we all need to know now that it is the brain that needs to be destroyed in order to stop a zombie. The brain being the zombie's Achilles heel. Although the brain isn't in the heel, it's actually in the area of your head which is that place above your shoulders with your face attached.... But if you needed to know that you really are beyond help... Okay! So we now we must destroy the...

Dale points at Tristen

TRISTEN: Brain

DALE: Because if you don't you'll end up...

Dale points at Donald. Donald just stares back at him.

DALE: Donald?

DONALD: Yes?

DALE: I pointed.

DONALD: Yes, no, I know, it's just I wasn't sure if you wanted me to say it or not because I was stood over there before and now you're pointing over here which is where you usually point if....

DALE: Donald, Donald, Donald, okay, right, it's fine, I can see why you'd get confused. Would it help if I pointed over here? (*Points at Position A / Judy*)

DONALD: Oh, yes, would you, that would be really helpful.

DALE: Okay. Fine.... If you don't destroy it you will end up...

Dale points at Position A / Judy - both Donald and Judy respond at the same time

DONALD: Dead

JUDY: Bitten

DALE: Judy, what are you doing?

JUDY: You pointed at me.

DALE: Yes, but I was asking for Donald. Donald was getting confused you see, so he needs me to point over here.

JUDY: But I'm likely to get confused if you point at me and mean Donald, I look nothing like Donald...

DALE: Well, right, fine. Why don't you move and find somewhere out there (*points at audience*)

JUDY: But Tristen is sat out there. Then that might get confusing, we won't know who you're pointing at.

TRISTEN: I won't get confused.

DALE: You won't get confused?

TRISTEN: No.

DALE: Right, well, why don't you come and stand here where Judy was (*points at POSITION A*) and Judy you go down there (*points at POSITION C*) Is that okay?

Tristen and Judy swap places so that Judy is now in position C and Tristen is in position A

JUDY: Yes, that's fine. I think I can cope with being mistaken for Tristen, he's younger.

DONALD: What are you saying?

DALE: Can we get on! Right! Everyone happy? Good. Let's get to rule four. Now rule four is the most important rule of all, it will help you map out your entire zombie survival plan. It will make you realise the answers to some difficult decisions that have to be made. It is the very epicentre of the survival movement because Rule number four is: There is no...

Dale holds his arms out to encompass Donald, Tristen and Judy

DONALD/TRISTEN/JUDY: Cure!

DALE: There is no...

Dale motions to all at once

DONALD/TRISTEN/JUDY: Cure!

The next segment is performed seamlessly at top speed with no pauses or breaks or confusion

DALE: So if someone is... (*Points at B - Donald*)

JUDY: Bitten

DALE: They will end up... (*Points at A - Tristen*)

DONALD: Dead

DALE: And you will have to destroy their... (*Points at C - Judy*)

TRISTEN: Brain

DALE: If you don't destroy their... (*Points at C - Judy*)

TRISTEN: Brain

DALE: Then you will end up... (*Points at B - Donald*)

JUDY: Bitten

DALE: And you will end up... (*Points at A - Judy*)

DONALD: Dead

DALE: Once you are... (*Points at A - Judy*)

DONALD: Dead

DALE: You will go around... (*Points at B - Tristen*)

JUDY: Biting

DALE: Other people until someone destroys your... (*Points at C - Judy*)

TRISTEN: Brain

DALE: Because there is no ... (***Motions to all***)

DONALD/TRISTEN/JUDY: Cure

DALE: Now I hope that's clear.

THE SIMULATION PART ONE (*The heading to this segment of the play might be displayed on an overhead projector or flip chart*)

DALE: Okay. So now we've discovered what kind of zombie we'll be up against I think it's time that we started to learn exactly how to......

An alarm begins to sound continually.

All on stage look concerned or worried. Tristen runs out of the room for a second and then returns to the stage.

Donald goes to a female member of the audience and tells her not to panic.

Dale and Judy discuss what the noise is.

Dale cuts the alarm off with a hand gesture.

DALE: What's that Judy?

JUDY: It's the zombie alarm.

DALE: The zombie alarm. What does that mean?

JUDY: It can mean only one thing! The zombie apocalypse has begun!

DALE: The zombie apocalypse has begun!

They all pose with shocked expressions on their faces. Then break it simultaneously.

DALE: But not really. You see what that alarm was, well, it was to signal to us the beginning of….

JUDY: Dr Dale.

DALE: Yes, Judy?

JUDY: Er… It's Donald.

DALE: Donald? (*spots Donald*) Donald! Donald!

DONALD: Oh, yes?

DALE: What are you doing?

DONALD: Well, the zombie apocalypse has begun, you know I was talking to this woman here and we were,…

DALE: Why?

DONALD: Well, you know, when the zombie apocalypse starts we need to start thinking about repopulation.

DALE: Donald, but you know this is just a simulation, right?

DONALD: Yes, but she doesn't.

DALE: Donald! Get back here!

Donald comes back to the stage

DALE: Yes, a simulation. That's what we're doing. It's no longer about teaching you how to survive we are also going to see which of you will survive. Through a series of questions posed to you, simulated situations and scenes presented to you whereby you have to make a decision, we will discover which of you would live and which of you would die. Now, obviously you may be wondering how we're going to do that, we can't just kill you as that would be wrong. But this is where the name stickers come in. We didn't give them to you so we could learn your names. Why on earth would we want to learn your names? No, the real reason is that if you are wearing your name badge then you are still alive. If you answer a question that is posed to you tonight incorrectly then you will remove your name tag and you will end up dead. If you make a wrong decision in one of the sequences we present to you, you will end up dead. If, during the Q & A segment you ask a stupid question you will remove your name sticker and you will end up dead. If you happen to have stood up at the beginning of the seminar and admitted to not caring about the zombie apocalypse then you will remove your name sticker and you will be dead.

Dale points at the person who the audience applauded in the intro

DALE: I'm afraid you're dead. Please remove your sticker.

The audience at this point usually respond with panto sympathy

DALE: No sympathy! This is a zombie apocalypse! Do you want me to kill you all too? No! There is no mercy in a zombie apocalypse. Our first victim tonight. Now, we've performed this show a few times and audiences have varied differently the best percentage that we've had survive is ____% and the worse is zero. So, it's not as easy as you think to score high. You've got to keep your wits about you to answer questions like.... Well, let's give it a shot. Just put your hand in the air. Who exercises two to three times a week? That's it! Just hands in the air, don't be worried. It's not a trap! See, you guys have a higher positive chance of survival. Much like Zombieland stated that Cardio is important. We agree. The fitter you are, the more likely you are to survive. Okay, has anyone else got any questions?

DONALD: Yes! Oh yes!

DALE: Okay, Donald, yes?

DONALD: Right, who here likes going camping?

DALE: Now, before you answer that remember there's a difference between who goes camping and who likes going camping.

DONALD: Put your hands up.

DALE: (*Surveys audience response*) Okay, that's good. If you like going camping then you have a higher positive chance of surviving the zombie apocalypse because you don't mind living in uncomfortable hellish conditions for periods of time without creature comforts. Anyone else?

TRISTEN: Er yes... Who here knows how to sail a boat?

DALE: Okay, good question, show of hands. Anyone know why that's important?

Take responses

DALE: It's because zombies can't swim. Yes, the thing is zombies can 'survive' underwater - there's inverted commas there around survive because they are not alive but because they don't need to breathe they can walk under water, but if you're in a boat they can't get to you, unless it's a swan peddle boat in a paddling pool, because that's quite shallow, so don't go for that. But a yacht or a cruise liner. Although cruise liners hold their own problems... mainly daily bingo and not being able to get a sun lounger by the pool because of fat Germans, but hey, it's the apocalypse you can club them to death. Okay, Judy?

JUDY: Who here is a vegetarian?

Wait for audience to put their hands up.

DALE: Dead. Yup, sorry, you're dead, I'm not kidding, remove your stickers. Yes! Vegetarians are not likely to survive the apocalypse. There is reasoning behind this. We don't just kill you off randomly, willy nilly. Problem with vegetarians is that there will be no supplements during a zombie apocalypse in order to keep their energy up, so they'll just be too weak. There are positives to keeping vegetarians around at the offset of the apocalypse. First off, if your group gets attacked you can just trip them up and use them to distract the zombies whilst you escape or secondly, they're usually so thin and bony that you can pick them up and use them as a spear or some form of club to fight the zombies off with. Okay! Excellent! So how many people are still alive?

Audience show

DALE: Okay, that's good! Doing well, so far.

IMMEDIATE REACTION (*The heading to this segment of the play might be displayed on an overhead projector or flip chart*)

During this segment if the audience shouts out ridiculous suggestions they can be killed immediately

DALE: Right let's get into the simulation properly! The alarm went off, the zombie apocalypse has started and we're all trapped in here. Now does anyone know what we should do? Feel free to shout out, and those of you who are already dead. You can still join in, you're not actually dead, you just took a sticker off. Okay, so ideas!

Takes suggestions from audience which, unless they match where the segment is going, are ridiculed.

DALE: Right, some interesting ideas there, but there are four important things that you need to remember when a zombie apocalypse begins which all centre around immediate reaction. Now the most important thing to do is stay here. If a zombie apocalypse is raging outside you don't want to run out into the middle of it and think about getting to your pesky loved ones or relatives. No, if they're smart, they will do exactly as you do. Hunker down and wait for the initial onslaught to end, wait for all the stupid people to die and the zombies to migrate off and find some other heavily populated area to cause carnage in. At that point - say three to four weeks we can think about leaving here and going and meeting up with our friends, loved ones, etc., unless they happen to be just like the stupid people and have ended up dead. So, we've followed the advice of Immediate Reaction and we're staying here. But there are four things we need to source can anyone name one of them?

Judy, Donald and Tristen get four A4 cards from the lectern. Each card has a letter that spells FAST. They stand in a line with the cards held to their chests without the letter on view. The cards are assigned as follows - Judy = F, Donald = A, Tristen = (Right Hand) S (Left Hand) T. The letters stand for Fortify, Arm, Sustenance and Team.

Once the first one has been guessed.

DALE: Okay, that's correct! Now to help you remember what these four . things are you need to remember we've created an acronym. Which is a word made from the first word of the other four words. So thus far we've got an ……. What else can you think of?

As each word is guessed the letter is revealed and Dr Dale asks the audience what in the building they are currently in they could use to complete each individual task.

This goes on until all four letters are revealed.

DALE: Okay, so there you have it. The acronym FAST. That means you've got to think FAST in a zombie apocalypse and it will help you survive. So before we move on, let's just remind ourselves what these four letters are.

JUDY: F – Fortify

DONALD: A - Arm

TRISTEN: S - Substenance, T - Team....

DALE: No, sorry, Tristen. It's sustenance.

TRISTEN: Substenance.

DALE: Sustenance.

TRISTEN: Sustenance

DALE: Substenance.

TRISTEN: Sustenance.

DALE: Right, sorry. Donald, what does this mean?

DONALD: Sustenance.

DALE: Okay, thanks. Donald, can you do that?

DONALD: Certainly.

As Dale apologises to the audience, Donald and Tristen swap places in the line up and also swap cards. Donald isn't happy with having two cards though and passes the S back to Tristen who now has A in his right hand and S in his left hand.

DALE: Okay, guys, sorry about that. We need to make sure we get it right. Don't want to confuse you in a zombie apocalypse not knowing how to think fast. Let's start again.

JUDY: F - Fortify

TRISTEN: A - Arm, S - Substanance....

DALE: Wait? What? I thought you were doing that Donald.

DONALD: I was, but I had too many cards...

DALE: Look, Judy, what does this stand for?

JUDY: Sustenance.

DALE: Right, excellent. Judy, you do S and T. Er..., Donald you come and do F. You know what it stands for don't you?

Donald moves and takes the F, Judy takes the S and T

DONALD: Yes.

DALE: Excellent. Right, sorry guys we'll move on in a second. Just need to make sure we get this right, though. We'll just go through it one more time. Donald.

DONALD: F - Fornicate.

DALE: Donald!

DONALD: What?

DALE: Fortify!

DONALD: Forty-five?

DALE: Fortify

DONALD: Fort-Five?

DALE: Fortify!

DONALD: Forty-five?

Dale snatches the card and gives it to Tristen.

DALE: Fortify

TRISTEN: Forty Six. Forty Seven

DALE: Tristen! Right, this? A is for -

TRISTEN: Apple.

DALE: Donald! A is for?

DONALD: Arm.

DALE: Right, you go in the middle.

JUDY: Who's going to do F?

DALE: You

TRISTEN: Umbrella.

DALE: A?

DONALD: Arm.

JUDY: S - Sustenance. T...

DALE: No, no, no, wait a minute... Tristen why did you say umbrella?

TRISTEN: You said U. U is for Umbrella.

DALE: Oh.

TRISTEN: Octopus

DALE: A?

DONALD: Arm

JUDY: S - sustenance, T...

DALE: Tristen! Whoa! Wait!

JUDY: Dr Dale, what's wrong? Why do you keep stopping us?

DALE: I don't think Tristen fully understands.

JUDY: Why?

TRISTEN: Yellow.

JUDY: A?

DONALD: Arm

JUDY: S - sustenance, T -

DALE: Tristen!

TRISTEN: What?

DALE: See!

TRISTEN: Cucumber

DALE: Grrrrrrr...

TRISTEN: Grrrrrilla?

DALE: Look, this is not difficult!! It's F - Fortify

DONALD: A - Arm

JUDY: S - Sustenance

Tristen grabs the final card

TRISTEN: T - Team!

DALE: Yes!

JUDY: I think we've got it. Can we move on.
DALE: Okay.

TRISTEN: Orange Kangaroo.

Dale throws Tristen a withering stare. The cards are put back on the lectern

THE SIMULATION PART TWO *(The heading to this segment of the play might be displayed on an overhead projector or flip chart)*

DALE: Okay, so now we know exactly what to do once the apocalypse begins let's find out how many more of you will survive. Any of the team got any questions?

TRISTEN: Who here has been a member of the scouts, guides, boys club, Brownies, *(list long number of youth clubs…)*

Audience put their hands up

DALE: Okay… that's good because….

TRISTEN: You know how to hold a bake sale.

DALE: And you are used to working as part of a team and also you'll be able to tie knots and have learnt various skills that will help with your survival. So, you guys have a higher chance of survival. Excellent. Anyone else?

JUDY: Who here is left handed?

DALE: Who here is left handed?

Audience put their hands up

DALE: Dead.

Audience reaction

DALE: Okay, again, I've nothing against left handed people, but the straight facts are that you are less likely to survive. The majority of implements that have been manufactured are for right handed people. So picture the scene - You're in your friend's kitchen, the apocalypse begins, your friend becomes a zombie and you want to protect yourself, you pick up a pair of scissors to stab them in the head and you can't quite use them properly because they are right handed scissors. There you are! Dead! Of course, I will allow you to put your sticker back on if you can effectively use both hands.

DONALD: Oh yes, I favour my left hand and so technically would be classed as left handed, but because I knew I'd have less of a chance of survival I've learnt how to use both hands.

DALE: Yes.

DONALD: So now I'm anorexic.

DALE: Ambidextrous.

DONALD: Bless you.

DALE: So, if you can use both hands then you can put your sticker back on, but be honest! If you are left handed and you lie about it, once the apocalypse begins and you're in your safe house with your team, if they find out later down the line that you are left handed then they will burn you as a witch. Okay! Right, next question. Who here knows martial arts?

Audience responds

DALE: Now, this is a difficult one - I'm not going to kill you, because I'm scared of you. No, I'm only joking, of course, but martial arts are so varied that it's hard to quantify how well you'd fare dependant on the martial arts form you practise. You see weapons based martial arts are good, but hand to hand forms tend to be bad. Now, the reason for this is... well, why don't we just show you...

HAND TO HAND DANCING *(The heading to this segment of the play might be displayed on an overhead projector or flip chart)*

DALE: ... Erm....Judy, could you be a small Japanese man?

Judy just crouches slightly.

DALE: Thank you, now we all know that the Japanese are experts at hand to hand martial arts and that those at the top of their game can break through blocks of concrete with their hands...

Judy mimes it

DALE: Their feet

Judy mimes it

DALE: Their heads

Judy mimes it

DALE: And their chests.

Judy does a chest thrust.

DALE: Okay, now imagine if a zombie came along. Donald can you be a zombie.

Donald changes his posture to be a zombie.

DALE: Thank you

Judy and Donald mime the next bit in slow motion as Dale narrates.

DALE: Now, here comes the zombie and Japanese Judy decides to kill it using her martial arts skills. We know we have to destroy the brain and her hand travels with speed in a downwards motion through the skull, but because of the force carries on travelling through the face and down to the mouth where her fingers get nicked on the teeth, which is technically classed as a bite. So, what we end up with is a small Japanese zombie.

Judy's mime of a Japanese zombie consists of a cross between a zombie and the karate kid pose (the one where he's on the beach)

DALE: So that's why hand to hand martial arts are a bad idea as you don't particularly want to go waving your hands around in front of a zombie's face. Thank you Judy. Now, if you don't have a weapon, and you do need to use hand to hand combat, there are certain methods that we at the School of Survival would sanction and I tell you what, we're running a bit ahead of schedule, maybe we could show you one of those now. Er... Tristen, do you want to do this?

TRISTEN: Yes!

DALE: Now Tristen has been learning some of the basic moves and I want you to teach the audience how to do something easy.

TRISTEN: Teach them?

DALE: Something they can take away with them tonight. So that if the zombie apocalypse does start then they've got a way of protecting themselves and they've felt like they've learnt something practical.

TRISTEN: Okay.. Er... one zombie?

DALE: Yep, sounds good.

TRISTEN: Okay, this is how to kill one zombie that's attacking you. Now first you want the zombie to see you as a potential target, so you raise your hands up so that you look prone in this area.

Tristen raises his arms in the Y position and then motions to his central area.

DALE: Now, this is especially useful if you're in a group and you want to protect someone else and draw the zombie away from them and towards you, because you will obviously know how to kill it. We believe zombies to be natural predators, so it is likely that they won't be opportunist killers, but will focus first on those they believe to be the easiest target, and as you are in this open position they should be drawn towards you.

TRISTEN: Once the zombie is within this area about three to four foot in front of you and within arm's reach (*Tristen motions the area*) you reach down and grab its ears, making sure your hands are away from the mouth.

Tristen brings his arms round to grab the ears of the imaginary zombie. It is an approximation of an M arm pose

DALE: Now, there will be those experts amongst you, out there, who will be thinking to yourselves, what happens if the zombie is rotten. The very nature of dead zombies is that they will rot and thus the ears may just come off in your hands and thus the zombie's head could keep moving forward and bite you in the face...

TRISTEN: Or boob.

Dale and Tristen adopt the M position

DALE: So, you'll need to use your judgement in this case, assess whether the zombie is likely to fall to pieces and instead of grabbing the ears adopt Position Two...

Dale and Tristen, holding the position, stick the index finger of each hand out as if they are grabbing the zombie by sticking their fingers in its ears.

DALE: Of course, that's a judgement call to be made at the time. Carry on Tristen

TRISTEN: Next, with a sharp sideways movement to the left we need to yank the zombie's head off.

Tristen pulls the head off, leaving the arms in the C position

TRISTEN: We pull the head off in this direction to try and avoid blood splatter getting on ourselves should it carry the infection. It won't splash you, but it will splash those around you and any drip will fall on your shoulder and not your head.

DALE: Finally, we don't just think we're done there as a head is still extremely dangerous. The head can still survive without the body so we need to make sure we finish the job.

TRISTEN: We swing our arms apart, making sure the zombie head is still held in either our left or right hand, your choice, and then bring them together with force,smushing the brain.

Tristen smushes the head in the A position above his head.

DALE: Of course, your personal strength and the level of decomposition of the zombie will depend on how easy that last move is and how many times you'll have to carry it out. Now, that's the simple way of doing it, but there was something missing and that was the noises. You see, when in battle it is important that you verbalise your intent. Generally speaking this was to scare away any potential attackers and undermine their confidence, but as zombies feel no fear, this should be more for your own confidence. To psych yourself up if you will and help you keep yourself motivated, not just for the physical battle, but the mental battle as well. So, Donald, give us an example of some of the noises that you might utilise.

Donald makes several grunts and moans that you might possibly associate with battle cries and some that you really wouldn't.

DALE: Donald is an expert at battle cries, he practises them daily.

DONALD: Oh yes.

TRISTEN: I hear him doing them in his room on his own late at night.

DALE: So, now, let's try putting all that together. Let's run through the moves and see if you've got it. Tristen, if you lead them first of all and feel free to verbalise with some battle cries.

Gestures to audience to stand. The audience follow Tristen's movements

TRISTEN: Okay, first we open ourselves up to the zombie, allowing it to come into our personal space, then once it's there we grab its ears, doing either position one or two, then we rip its head off keeping the blood splatter away from ourselves and then we smash in its head!

DALE: Okay, good, most of you seem to have got it, but now let's try it just on your own to make sure that you've got it ingrained in your brain. Okay, so let's imagine a zombie is coming towards it and let's kill it!

The audience carry out the move without being led.

DALE: Okay, that was good, Tristen what do you think?

TRISTEN: Well, they were good, but that guy looked like he was being attacked by a big hairy bumble bee.

DALE: Okay, that's okay. Not everyone is going to get it first time, and I'm sure they will want to go away and practise, but at least they've learnt something practical today and the thing is, you may not need to put it into practice until many years down the line, but there could be a time when the zombie apocalypse has begun and you find yourself faced with a zombie and you think to yourself. 'Oh no! I need to defend myself, what was that move that Dr Dale taught me?' Well don't worry as there's a very easy way to instantly recall the move so you remember it and that is…

TRISTEN does the individual moves as Dale speaks

DALE: Y M C A. In fact, we have discovered that most dance moves can be utilised in protecting yourself from the undead.

Tristen does the moves

DALE: If you've got several zombies attacking you - Agadoo.

Tristen does the push pineapples shake the tree part of the song

DALE: If you're being attacked at either side by an adult zombie and a child zombie - Staying Alive

Tristen does the John Travolta point up point down move

DALE: And if you do get bitten. Tragedy.

Tristen does the hands around the head bit of the dance.

DALE: Okay, well now we've gone through that, I think it's the perfect opportunity to take a breather after all that rigorous exercise and go into the Q & A - this is the part of the seminar when you can ask us anything you want about the zombie apocalypse. Just put your hand in the air and we'll see if we can help you out.

QUESTION AND ANSWER SESSION (*The heading to this segment of the play might be displayed on an overhead projector or flip chart*)

Usually in an hour long show there is time to answer three or four questions

THE SIMULATION PART 3 *(The heading to this segment of the play might be displayed on an overhead projector or flip chart)*

DALE: Okay, well let's move on, and what better way to segway into the next part of the show by killing a few more of you off. Any questions?

JUDY: Who here can swim under water, but keep their eyes open when they do so?

Audience hands up

DALE: Okay, well, we should already know why this is a good thing. We know that zombies can't swim, but they can 'survive' under water. So, if a zombie has got trapped under water and you need to cross that expanse, you'll need to keep an eye out for anything that might reach up and pull you under. Okay good.

DONALD: Who here is _____ *(fill the blank with any current unpopular group that you wish)*

Audience reaction

DALE: Dead! Okay, if you need a reason, we just don't like you. If the zombies don't kill you, we'll kill you ourselves. Any other questions?

JUDY: Who here knows who they would take with them on their team?

BLIND DATE *(The heading to this segment of the play might be displayed on an overhead projector or flip chart)*

Tristen, Judy and Donald put three chairs in a row in the centre of the stage and sit on them in the order of Right - Donald, Centre - Judy, Left - Tristen

DALE: Okay, you seem pretty confident in that choice. But you've made that decision on people that you already know. That you are already aware of. But remember, some of those people might not be with you today. Some of those people might already be dead, and we have to bear in mind the situation that we are currently in. We're all here in this building thinking fast. So after the three or four weeks are up and we decide we want to move on we could potentially team up with people in here. People who we've met today, just take a look around you, these are the people you'll be spending three or four weeks with. Can you sum up with an initial assumption who would be good and who would be bad to take with you in a zombie apocalypse out of the people in this room? Well, let's test that theory, I'm just going to pick someone.

Dale picks a man from the audience

DALE: Okay, just stand up for me, sir. *(Man stands up)*

DALE: Now, don't be scared, I'm not going to ask you to do anything embarrassing, all I'm going to do is ask you to stand there and I want the rest of the audience to look at you. Now, from a show of hands, I want everyone to make a split decision, just looking at this guy, would you take him with you on your team in a zombie apocalypse? Just make a decision on looking at him and put your hands in the air. Okay, but I want you to keep your hands in the air and I'm going to ask you a question, sir. Now, I just want a one word answer from you, split second decision, no reasoning behind your answer. I want you to tell me which one of my team you would decide to take with you in a zombie apocalypse. Is it Donald, Judy or Tristen? One word answer please.

Audience member gives his answer

DALE: Okay, any of you who originally picked him want to change your mind now? Okay, a couple at the back there, some down here, oh, and a couple have put their hands up. Okay sir, thank you, you can sit down. Now what that tells us is that just by looking at him you made a decision on whether to take him, then on hearing his answer to one question some of you changed your minds. Now, that just proves that you can't always trust your first impressions, but sometimes in a zombie apocalypse you'll have to completely rely on them. So, this next exercise tests whether you can pick the perfect team member just by meeting them and hearing the answer to one question. That question being, which of the other two would they take if they had the opportunity? Now this is part of the simulation, there is a correct answer of one being better than the others, so if you pick the correct one you will stay alive, if you pick one of the other two you will end up dead. But! And this is a big but. And we like big buts we cannot lie. They won't be playing themselves. We won't be interviewing my actual team, as you've already had more than enough opportunity to assess them and decide who you would take... just out of interest, and this isn't part of the simulation I won't kill you if you give the wrong answer, who would you have chosen if it had been these three? Who would have taken Donald?

Show of hands

DALE: Who would have taken Judy?

Show of hands

DALE: Who would have taken Tristen?

Show of hands

DALE: You're lucky it wasn't part of the simulation. But no, that doesn't count as we want this to be based on first impressions, so I gave the team a piece of paper with a character synopsis on for them to play today and it's those characters that you have to choose between remember one of them will keep you alive, two will help you end up dead. Okay, so pay attention as we meet the characters.

DONALD: (*Upper Class*) Hello, I'm Robert Posenby-Smythe. I am very good at working with teams, in fact I'm very good at leading teams. Yes, yes I am, hah!

DALE: Thank you, Robert. Next up.

JUDY: (*chav*) 'Ello, my names Courtney, and I think I'd be great in the apocalypse cos I've got kids.

DALE: How many?

JUDY: Seventy four, innit.

DALE: Thank you... and finally...

TRISTEN: Hello, my name's Tristen, I work at the School of Survival and Dr Dale's my uncle..

DALE: No, Tristen, what are you doing?

TRISTEN: Introducing myself.

DALE: No, you're supposed to be playing a character...

TRISTEN: What?

DALE: I gave you a piece of paper with a character written on it.

Tristen looks blankly at him

DALE: Where's the piece of paper?

TRISTEN: I got hungry.

DALE: You ate it...

Tristen nods slowly

DALE: Right, well, it doesn't matter, just make a character up.

TRISTEN: How?

DALE: Just change your voice.

TRISTEN: What?

DALE: Like Donald and Judy.

Donald and Judy demonstrate by making various random vowel sounds in their character voices.

TRISTEN: I'm not very good with voices.

DALE: Well, just copy someone... er... you, sir!

Points at someone in the audience who looks like he might have a gruff voice.

DALE: Sir, could you just say hello.

AUDIENT: Hello.

DALE: There, copy that.

TRISTEN: (*going gruff*) Hello

DALE: Do it again.

AUDIENT: Hello...

TRISTEN: (*getting gruffer*) Hello

DALE: One more time.

AUDIENT: Hello.

TRISTEN: (*gruffer still*) Hello.

DALE: Okay, good - now create a character using that voice.

Tristen thinks for a second and then does a pirate pose brandishing his cutlass.

TRISTEN: I'm a pirate!

DALE: No! You can't be a pirate.

TRISTEN: Why?

DALE: Because this is a sensible exercise...

TRISTEN: You told me to copy him!

DALE: Yes, but....

TRISTEN: It's not my fault he's a pirate!

DALE: He's not a pirate!

TRISTEN: He's not?

DALE: No!

TRISTEN: This is just like the time Judy said Santa didn't exist.

DALE: Judy!

JUDY: I didn't say he didn't exist. I said he was dead.

DALE: Right, different thing, but you can't be a pirate.

TRISTEN: I can do Welsh!

DALE: Well be Welsh.

TRISTEN: (*worst Welsh accent in the world*) Hello! My name is Mr Welsh.

Dale just stares at him for a moment

DALE: Just be a pirate.

TRISTEN: Yay!(*becomes a pirate*) Arrrgh!!!

JUDY: Hey! That's not fair!

DONALD: I don't agree with this!

DALE: What?

JUDY: How come he gets to be a pirate and I get stuck being Courtney.

DONALD: Yeah, our characters are boring.

DALE: I need you to be sensible characters!

JUDY: Well I think it's unfair.

DONALD: Yes, if you don't let us change our characters I'm leaving.

JUDY: Me too!

Donald and Judy stand up to leave

DALE: Right! Fine! You can change your characters!

JUDY: Thank you.
DONALD: Good.

Donald and Judy sit back down.

DALE: We'll just have to improvise through it. Okay, right, sorry everyone, we're going to start again. Same premise. I'm going to introduce three characters to you and you are going to assess them on your first impressions and listen to the answer to the question as to which of the other two they would take and then chose which one you would take. Remember only one will keep you alive. Two of them will make you end up dead. Okay, so let's start again and meet the characters.

TRISTEN: I'm a pirate!

JUDY: I'm a pirate!

DONALD: I'm a pirate! (*must brandish his cutlass left-handed*)

DALE: No! You can't all be pirates!

JUDY: Why not?

DALE: Because otherwise the choice would be a pirate, a pirate or a pirate. I shall allow one pirate.

DONALD: Oh me!

DALE: Right, Donald is the pirate.

JUDY/TRISTEN: That's not fair!

DALE: Donald put his hand up first!

TRISTEN: But I was the pirate first!

DONALD: Okay, right, well, we'll do this fairly. We'll play the numbers game. Tristen, think of a number between one and ten.

TRISTEN: Three.

DALE: Judy?

JUDY: Nine.

DALE: Donald?

DONALD: Six

DALE: Okay, there we go, Donald wins. He's the pirate.

TRISTEN: But what can I be?

DALE: Just pick another character.

TRISTEN: Oh! I know! I'll be a dinosaur!

DALE: A dinosaur.

TRISTEN: Oh! No! No! A Predator!

Tristen mimes being a predator by just hissing through spider fingers on his face.

DALE: Okay, a predator and Judy?

JUDY: I'm going to be the Pope.

Creates pope hat with her arms

DALE: Which one?

JUDY: Pope John Paul the Second

DALE: Right, okay. Fine. So let's get this started. You now have to make the decision which of these three normal everyday people you would have on your team. So I am now going to ask them one question. That question being, hypothetically speaking, if they could take one of the other two with them on their team, which one would they take. Remember, one of them is the right answer, two of them will kill you. So, pirate, you first!

Donald takes on his pirate character using his left arm to brandish his sword

DONALD: Arrrgh!

DALE: Given the choice, which of the other two would you take with you in a zombie apocalypse?

DONALD: Oh, I would take the dinosaur, arrrgh!

DALE: Donald, there is no dinosaur.

DONALD: (*dropping character*) Yes! Tristen said he was going to be a dinosaur.

DALE: No, he changed his mind.

TRISTEN: I can be a dinosaur if you want...

DALE: No, he doesn't...

TRISTEN: I can do a very good dinosaur

Tristen does a T-Rex impression

DONALD: Well, if we're holding auditions I can do a dinosaur too!

Donald does a T-Rex Impression - Dale tries to shut them up

They continue doing dinosaur impressions

Judy does an impression of a squawking dinosaur, using her hands as its head flaps

The other three stop and watch her

There is a pause

Everyone agrees that Judy does a great dinosaur

TRISTEN: That was great!

DONALD: Best dinosaur I've seen.

DALE: Okay, Judy can be the dinosaur.

JUDY: Oh no, I'm happy being the Pope.

DALE: But the pirate wants to take a dinosaur.

JUDY: Yes, but I'm the Pope.

TRISTEN: Donald could be the Pope.

DONALD: Oh yes!

DALE: See, Donald could be the Pope.

JUDY: Please don't take the Pope away from me!

DALE: Er... well, could you be the dinosaur and the Pope?

JUDY: I suppose I could overlook the theological inconsistencies.

DALE: Right.

DONALD: Oh! Does that mean I'm not the Pope!

DALE: You're the pirate!

DONALD: But I've always wanted to be the Pope.

DALE: Yes, but Judy picked the Pope first, you got to be the pirate.
DONALD: I'll tell you what, let's do the numbers game.

DALE: Right fine.

DONALD: Think of a number.

DALE: Nine.

DONALD: Two! Ha!

DALE: Darn it! Right, Donald's the Pope.

JUDY: But I'm the Pope!

DALE: There are enough Popes to go round. He can be Pope Benedict, you can be Pope John Paul the Second.

TRISTEN: If there are enough Popes to go round, why can't I be the Pope!

DALE: Do you even know who the Pope is?

TRISTEN: Yes! (*puts his hand on his head like a telly tubby and does telly tubby impression*) Eh oh!

DALE: That's Po.

TRISTEN: Oh... Well, it's still not fair! They get to be two characters.

DALE: Well, pick another character.

TRISTEN: A predator.

DALE: You're already a predator.

TRISTEN: Another predator.

DALE: No.

TRISTEN: A transformer!

DONALD: You want to be a woman?

DALE: Transformer, not transgender.

TRISTEN: Like Skids, Mudflap or Jazz.

DONALD: Really?

TRISTEN: No, not wheelie. Skids, Mudflap or Jazz.

DONALD: What?
TRISTEN: Skids, Mudflap or Jazz.

DALE: Will you stop saying that! It sounds like bad porn.

TRISTEN: So not a transformer. Oh! Oh! Oh! I could be a vampire!

Makes his fingers into his fangs

DALE: A vampire.

TRISTEN: Yes.

DALE: Right, fine, now can we get on. I'll start again, ask the question, get the answer, you choose, make the right choice. Okay! Pirate, who would you take?

DONALD: Arrgh, the dinosaur.

DALE: Right, Pope John Paul, who would you take?

JUDY: I would take the predator.

DALE: Predator, who would you take?

TRISTEN: (*hisses like a predator*)

DALE: (*looks at him with disdain*) Right, Pope Benedict, who would you take?

DONALD: I would take the other Pope.

DALE: Dinosaur, who would you take?

Dinosaur: I would take the predator.

DALE: And vampire, who would you take?

As Tristen has his fingers in his mouth as fangs he can't speak properly.

TRISTEN: The Pope.

DALE: The goat?

TRISTEN: Pope!

DALE: A ghost?

TRISTEN: The Pope!

DALE: No, I'm not getting it.

TRISTEN (*sighs*) The pirate.

DALE: Okay! The pirate! Right, so now we've met all the characters and we know who they would choose to take if they were given the chance. Now it's down to you. You can only pick one of these characters to have on your team. Choose carefully as only one of them will keep you alive...... Five of them will kill you.

Dependant on how many people are left alive at this point Dale can offer to let the people who are already dead take part and if no-one else survives he will bring them back to life. This ensures that you have people alive at the end of the show for the final game.

Dale gets a show of hands for each choice going through in the order he interviewed them. When he gets to the vampire he makes those who chose the vampire stand up.

DALE: Okay, if you are stood up then you are alive. If you are still sat down you are dead. The Vampire was the correct choice! Now, of course, it wasn't just a random choice, there was a reason why the vampire was the correct choice and I'll go through that now.

First off who chose the pirate? Not a bad choice. Pirates have their own boats and we've already said that boats are a good place to be, so the pirate would have been the second best choice. Problem with pirates is that they are very much into the looting and pillaging and if you get on the wrong side of them then they might be liable to loot and pillage you.

They're not exceptionally good team players, so it is likely that, rather than them becoming part of your team, you would have to become part of their team and their methods may be less than moral.

It really does depend what kind of person you want to be in an apocalypse as to who you join with, and if you do want to live the immoral life of a pirate then that's fine, I'm not going to judge you, but do remember, piracy is a crime and it is destroying the film and television industry. Do you want to be part of that? Besides, we weren't just assessing the answers that the characters gave, we were also assessing them personally and this pirate was a bad choice because... (*Donald brandishes his cutlass*). He is left-handed.

Okay, moving on. Why was the dinosaur a bad choice? Well, to be honest, some dinosaurs might be a good choice, some might be a bad choice, but I think from Judy's impersonation,

Judy does her impression

DALE: We all realised that this particular dinosaur was a Coahuilaceratops which is a herbivore, and we've already spoken of vegetarians, haven't we.

Next up the predator, now a predator might seem like a really good idea what with him having all his weapons, but why would a predator even be on our planet at the time of a zombie apocalypse? They are only interested in the challenge of the hunt and in an apocalypse there will only be two things they could hunt. Millions of disorganised, shambling zombies or a few straggly undernourished humans with spoons and tin foil for weapons. Neither of which would be a particular challenge for the predator.

The other problem is that they are not going to want to work with you. Despite the obvious communication problems you will have in talking to a predator, unless you've taken an online course in Predanese. They are notorious for working alone and surviving is all about team work.

Now, there will be those of you out there who say, hey, Dr Dale, you say that they won't want to work with us but what about the movie Aliens Versus Predator, they worked with us in that! And I would say, yes, yes they did, but Aliens Versus Predator was crap.

Okay. Moving on, I'm going to do both Popes together. Who chose the Pope?

Show of hands

DALE: Frankly, that was a ridiculous choice. Why on earth would you choose to take a fictional character? So finally to the correct choice. Why chose the vampire? Well, first off, it's easy to communicate with vampires. They did used to be human so we can physically talk to them and ensure a vibrant line of communication is open. Secondly, they cannot be infected by the zombie virus as they are already dead, they have no blood flow and therefore the infection won't be carried through the blood stream so they are immune so can get up close to zombies and use their enhanced strength to dispose of them. Talking of enhanced senses, they can also tell through smell or hearing where other living humans are so you can use them to either avoid or join with other camps easily increasing your own numbers to increase your own chance of survival.

Now, there will be those of you who may see a problem with this, in the fact that vampires drink human blood and could be a danger to us, but that is just the point. That is exactly why a vampire would work with humans in a zombie apocalypse.

What would happen if the zombies won in an apocalypse? There would be no more humans. If there were no more humans, there would be no more food for vampires and the vampire race would also die out. It's all about mutual benefit. Both of our species would need the zombies to be destroyed and vampires are intelligent enough to realise that and work with us in an apocalypse.

Now to make sure the vampire doesn't eat a member of your team is where vegetarians and stupid people come in. Always make sure you have someone on your team who you can tie in your basement in order that the vampire can feed off without actually killing them, just to keep them alive and happy to work with you without turning on anyone else. Now, I'm not saying that after the apocalypse you should carry on being friends with the vampire as things will more than likely change back to our normal way of life with them hunting us, so don't exchange phone numbers and get together on holidays or anything like that. Of course, there are some vampires that are better to have on your team than others. This vampire was just a standard vampire, but if you're lucky enough you could get Blade.

TRISTEN: Or Angel.

DALE: Or Angel, yes. However, under no circumstances join forces with a vampire who sparkles in the sunlight because frankly they're a waste of time. Okay! So, how many people are left alive?

Show of hands

DALE: Right, well, that's usually what we're more used to. See, it's not easy surviving a zombie apocalypse. Now, Judy, what time is it? Have we got time for one more segment?

JUDY: Yes, I think we have

COUNSELLING (*The heading to this segment of the play might be displayed on an overhead projector or flip chart*)

DALE: Okay, well, we're going to leave off killing any more of you for the moment as there's not that very many of you left. But the fact that so many of you have died brings up an interesting point.

The team add the Fourth chair to the row and Dale and Judy sit on the centre two.

DALE: Surviving the zombie apocalypse is not all about physical strength and prowess, it's also about having a strong mental ability as well and with all the death, pain and destruction that is going to surround you during a zombie apocalypse you may end up with members of your team who are teetering on the edge of sanity and this can be a problem. It could lead to someone becoming highly unstable and claustrophobic, dismantling the barricades and running outside in their underwear thus letting all the zombies in to devour you all. It could also lead to them becoming disorientated and paranoid and rather than opening the door they will just kill everyone in here with a spoon. You need to make sure that that is avoided and how do we do that? Judy?

JUDY: Counselling.

DALE: Counselling! Now surely to have the skills to be a counsellor, you would need years of training, some form of degree maybe and definitely have spent time in a higher learning institute.

JUDY: No.

DALE: Okay, so what you're saying is that frankly any idiot can do it?

JUDY: Yes.

DALE: Right, well maybe you'd like to fill us in a little bit about how to overcome mental problems in the team.

JUDY: Well, first off it's not just about being able to deal with the problem. It's also about being able to spot the problem. It is unlikely that anyone will come to you and say they are having mental issues and if you approach them and ask if everything is all right, they are likely to respond in the affirmative. It's human nature.

DALE: Okay, so how do we spot the problem?

JUDY: Well, if I can use Donald and Tristen to demonstrate.

Donald and Tristen move to stand FSR and FSL

JUDY: It's all about body language and facial expressions. You have to be able to spot even the tiniest tic or change in a person to realise what emotions they are going through.

DALE: And what are some of these negative emotions?

As Judy and Dale list the emotions, Tristen and Donald show them facially and physically. Initially Judy and Dale are quite methodical in listing the emotions, but they do speed up so Tristen and Donald have to speed up the changes in posture and expression.

JUDY: Well the most obvious are fear, anger and depression.

DALE: Fear, anger and depression?

JUDY: More minor ones are hate, shame and inferiority.

DALE: So, fear, anger, depression, hate, shame and inferiority.

JUDY: Yes.

DALE: Now, it would be lax of us just to quantify each individual emotion as purely fear, anger, depression, hate, shame and inferiority. Surely there are varying degrees.

JUDY: Oh yes, take fear for example. There are five distinct levels of fear that vary in degrees of seriousness. There's level one, level two, level three, level four and level five.

DALE: And those classes are for all emotions?

JUDY: Oh yes.

DALE: Now anger, depression, hate, shame, inferiority and fear level one, two, three, four and five are all negative emotions. Are there any positive emotions that can cause problems in a zombie apocalypse?

JUDY: Oh yes. Sometimes in times of stress people have been known to suffer from extreme arousal.

Donald and Tristen pull faces that couldn't be further from extreme arousal.

DALE: Okay, now we've got some idea of how to spot the problem, how do we deal with it?

JUDY: Well, we can do this by either choosing to carry out a one on one counselling method or a group exercise.

DALE: Okay, well, let's see an example of each. Maybe a one on one first.

JUDY: Okay.

DALE: Right, so Tristen, if you could pretend to be someone who has some form of mental problems and Judy will show how to cure you.

Dale stands and Tristen sits where Dale was

TRISTEN: What problem should I have?

DALE: Erm, okay, let's imagine that you're feeling distraught because you've had to kill your own mother.

Tristen starts to look upset

DALE: Hey, Tristen, don't worry, we're only pretending. You wouldn't really have to kill her, would you? Cos she's already dead. Okay, Judy, what technique are you going to use?

JUDY: I'm going to use one of my personal favourites called 'The Silent Treatment'

DALE: Okay, well let's take a look at that. Off we go.

Dale moves to one side. As Tristen tells his story, Judy just nods and looks interested or concerned throughout. Tristen begins very upset

TRISTEN: Well, Judy, it was mum's birthday, so I was cooking her a nice meal. Spaghetti Bolognaise, that's her favourite, but I'd run out of mushrooms, so I sent her to the shop. She likes a walk every now and again. So, I put the radio on and I continued cooking, then, all of a sudden, on the radio it said, the zombie apocalypse has begun. Oh no! What do I do! Well, I carried on cooking, then ten minutes later my mum came through the door and she was bleeding. She had a bite on her arm and I didn't know what to do. I said, 'Oh Mum. You've ruined your tea' So anyway, I sat her down in her chair, and I set the table up really nice and I lit a candle in front of her and laid the food out in front of her and then all of a sudden she started to... fade away. You could see it. She was going. So I got my knife and fork and stabbed them through her hands onto the table so she couldn't move. Then I moved the candle under her chin so it would slowly melt away through her head to her brain, and it did and it was an awful mess and my mum doesn't like mess, so I had to get a carving knife and chop her body into tiny bits and put her in a bin bag, but then when I went outside I didn't know what bin to put her in! Is it the black one or the green one? It's so confusing Judy!

Judy nods and smiles

Tristen calms down

TRISTEN: Yes, I suppose you're right. It didn't matter what bin I put her in. I had to do it. Oh thank you Judy, you've made it all so clear.

DALE: So there you go. You cured Tristen there, and for those of you who missed the transition of where the cure took place let's see it again in slow motion.

Tristen replays going from a sad face to a happy face in slow motion

DALE: There it is! But Judy, you didn't seem to say anything.

JUDY: No, I just nodded and shook my head and made the appropriate facial expressions.

DALE: So were you actually listening to anything he said?

JUDY: Oh God, no.

DALE: What were you actually thinking about.

JUDY: What I was going to have for tea tonight.

DALE: Which is?

JUDY: Lasagne.

TRISTEN: Oh, can I have some?

JUDY: No! You killed your mum.

DALE: Right, so that's the one on one, but you also spoke of group counselling.

JUDY: Or positive guided meditation.

DALE: I'm sure that's more interesting than it sounds.

JUDY: Yes, it is. You see the one on one counselling I just demonstrated is a curative measure whereas positive guided meditation can act as a preventative measure. Carried out once or twice a day with the whole team it can ensure that no mental problems manifest at all and keep everyone cool, calm and focused on the task in hand which is surviving.

DALE: Okay, well let's see this at work, then.

JUDY: Well, for this I'll need to use some volunteers.

DALE: Okay, well I'm sure Tristen and Donald will be happy to help.

Donald and Tristen sit in the centre two chairs of the row of four. Tristen on the R, Donald on the L

JUDY: I could do with just a couple more.
DALE: Okay, well that's not a problem, we'll just get some folks from the team

Dale picks two audience members - it is always preferable if they are male. They sit in the two empty chairs at the end of each row.

DALE: (*To each volunteer*) Okay, so what's your name. (*volunteers answer*) Okay, now this is technically a relaxation exercise so what would be great is if we can get a gauge on how it works. With that in mind could you let me know how stressed you are currently feeling on a scale of one to ten with ten being a high stress level. *(volunteers answer and react)*

DALE: Okay - so, that's your task Judy, lower those two stress levels, think you're up for it?

JUDY: Oh yes.

DALE: Right, well, I'll leave you to it. Just a quick note to the rest of the team. Obviously, this particular exercise does require a certain amount of silence so if you could just respect that it would be great. Some of you can take part from where you're sat and let Judy take you on a relaxing journey or others of you may want to watch and take notes and let Judy's wisdom wash over you. Okay, Judy over to you. (*Dale exits*)

JUDY: Okay, now first off I want the four of you to close your eyes and take a big, deep breath in and then a big deep breath out. (*Pause*) Then another big deep breath in and another big deep breath out. Now, keep breathing regularly because we're going to go on a journey. A beautiful, relaxing journey. I want you to imagine yourself in a boat, a boat that's in the middle of a beautiful blue ocean, sailing under beautiful clear skies towards a peaceful tropical island.

Donald begins to fall asleep. His head rests on the shoulder of the person sat next to him.

JUDY: Now, I want you to imagine that the boat has reached the island and you climb out of the boat. You can feel the soft, warm sand between your toes....

TRISTEN: I don't like the feeling of sand between my toes.

JUDY: It's okay. You're wearing Crocs.

TRISTEN: Oh! What colour?

JUDY: Blue.

TRISTEN: I don't like blue.

Judy gets more infuriated

JUDY: Orange.

TRISTEN: I don't like orange.

JUDY: Green

TRISTEN: I don't like green

JUDY: Red

TRISTEN: I don't like red.

JUDY: Well, what colour do you like?

TRISTEN: Blue

JUDY: Okay, they're blue! (*realises that she is getting angry and calms down*) So, we're walking along the beautiful, sandy beach with the sun shining down on us and we see a small oasis ahead.

Donald gets more comfy and puts his arm around the volunteer and snuggles in close

JUDY: It has lush green grass, and palm trees, and a pool of crystal-clear blue water. Everything is wonderful, everything is calm, everything is peaceful and relaxing.

Tristen screams and grabs the leg of the person next to him.

JUDY: What is it?

TRISTEN: A coconut just flew past my head and nearly hit me.

Judy begins to get irate and aggressive again

JUDY: No it didn't.

TRISTEN: It did. I just saw it!

JUDY: You're imagining it. There are no coconuts.

TRISTEN: No I'm not! (*referencing volunteer*) He saw it! Didn't you?

JUDY: He didn't see anything did you?

Volunteer generally says no at this point.

TRISTEN: He's lying! Poo head.

Judy calms herself down again

JUDY: It's just a calm, peaceful, relaxing oasis, with coconut free palm trees and a beautiful crystal-clear pool of water...

Donald puts his legs up on the lap of the volunteer next to him - getting really comfy now.

JUDY: ...It has lush green grass and lots of brightly coloured flowers that sway in the gentle breeze as the sun washes a warm feeling of calm across your entire body. You've never felt so at peace with the world, never felt so content...

TRISTEN: Er.... Judy....

JUDY: What is it Tristen?

TRISTEN: Something just moved behind that palm tree.

JUDY: No it didn't.

TRISTEN: It did, Judy. Oh no, Judy no...

Judy gets more irate again

JUDY: Tristen.

TRISTEN: Zombie!!!!!!

Tristen and Judy now talk over each other as Tristen gets more in a panic and Judy attempts to calm him down but gets more infuriated herself.

(TRISTEN: Quick! Run! Run for your life! (*grabs his volunteer's hand and mimes running*) Run! Run back to the beach! Quick before it gets us. Quick! Quick! The boats gone! Into the water, quick run!)

(JUDY: Tristen! Stop it! There is no zombie! This is a calm tranquil island! Tristen, calm down, Can you just stop it for one second and take a deep breath again, there is no zombie!

(TRISTEN: Oh no...... Piranha 3D!!!) (*begins weeping in terror and hyperventilating*)

JUDY: Listen there is no zombie! There is no piranha! This is a calm, tranquil island! Everything is beautiful! We're all relaxed! We're all calm! (*To Tristen's volunteer*) You're calm aren't you?

VOLUNTEER: Yes

JUDY: Well say it then! I am calm!!!

VOLUNTEER: I am calm!

JUDY: (*Less calmly.*) Say it like you mean it!!!!

VOLUNTEER: I am calm!

JUDY: (*Even less calmly*) Put some goddamn effort in!

VOLUNTEER: I am calm!

JUDY: I am caaaaaaaaaaaaaalmmmmmmmmmmm!!!!!!

Dale enters

DALE: And we're all relaxed.

DALE: (*To Tristen's volunteer*) Okay! So you said you were a stress level (-) before the exercise. Where would you say you are now?

If the volunteer puts his stress level as higher Judy gets up close to his ear and snarls

JUDY: You might want to rethink that number.

This usually gets the audience member to drop their number

DALE: Wow, excellent! Well, thank you for taking part. Give him a round of applause.

Audience member sits back in audience. Dale makes his way towards Donald's volunteer

DALE: Oh wow! Look at you, without even asking I can see that you've been touched by the exercise. You are positively glowing! Your stress level was (-). Where would you say you are now?

This volunteer usually gives a lower number, but if not, then Dale adds a minus to the number they give

DALE: (*Sounding impressed*) Well, that is fantastic. Thank you so much for taking part, you certainly got your moneys' worth from the ticket price today!

Audience member sits back in audience

DALE: So there we go, a couple of ways to keep your team on an even keel as you sail through the choppy waters of the zombie apocalypse on the good ship team work. But now, sadly, I think we've reached the end of our time with you, but before we go, there is one last thing that must be done and that is to see just how many of you have still got your stickers on and managed to survive. Don't just put your hands up, let's have you stood up and let's give them a round of applause. These guys have ensured that not only they will survive, but that you as an audience didn't fail miserably by having no survivors at all tonight. But! Before we go, I have one last question for you. Not for all of you, just the survivors. Now it's at this point in the proceedings that we ask the ultimate survivor question. Now, don't worry, if you get this question wrong then you don't die. You did survive until the end of the seminar, so we're not going to take that away from you. No, this question reaps its own reward. You see, in the history of this seminar, having been performed over 100 times around the world, only two people have ever got this question right. If you get this question right, you will be crowned the ultimate survivor and I will bring back to life everyone in this room meaning that you will have one of the highest audience survival rates of all time. So, are you ready for the challenge? Good.

Judy and Donald pick up the FAST letters from the lectern and hold them as before, spelling FAST.

THE ULTIMATE SURVIVOR (*The heading to this segment of the play might be displayed on an overhead projector or flip chart*)

This is scripted for the longest possible variation of the show - if no-one gets the answer at all. If someone does get the answer (which has only ever happened twice) then adapt as necessary.

DALE: Now, earlier, we told you that in a zombie apocalypse you should 'Think Fast' this is wrong! We lied to you! Terrible, I know. But there is a letter missing from this acronym. One other thing you should do at the beginning of a zombie apocalypse to ensure your survival. What I want from you, is the missing letter and what it stands for. Remember that the acronym must spell a word, but you can shuffle the letters around to make it.

Dale asks each of the survivors for their answer.

DALE: Okay, I tell you what, I'm feeling charitable. I'll help you out.

Whoever is holding the S and T swaps them round and sidesteps so the lectern is in between the letters A and T so now it spells FA-TS

DALE: Okay, the missing letter goes in here and I'm going to give you all one more chance to guess. What is the missing letter and what does it stand for?

Dale allows each survivor one more guess. Someone invariably guesses R giving Dale the opportunity to deride them for not taking the exercise seriously.

DALE: Okay, unfortunately you didn't get the ultimate survivor question right. Don't worry, you still survived, but now I'm going to put the question to the rest of the team.

Takes a few shout outs

DALE: Okay, let me help you out. Can anyone remember what happened when the zombie alarm went off?

Takes shout outs

DALE: Me and Judy stood on the stage talking, Donald went into the audience. Where did Tristen go? He went outside to see if the apocalypse had started, so what should we have done when he came back in? We should have checked him for bites. The missing letter is C for Check. Tristen, did you get bitten when you went outside?

TRISTEN: Yes

DALE: So, because we didn't check him, this is what would have happened.

Tristen looks ill, crumples down onto a chair and dies. After a moment he leaps up, roars and dives at a lady in the front row as if he is going to bite her.

Dale pulls a gun of the lectern and shoots him.

Tristen drops to the floor dead.

DALE: And I might not always be there to save your skin. Yes, you should always check everyone in the room for bites. We don't know how long it would take for the infection to take hold, so someone in this room could have been bitten hours before the apocalypse began and once we've barricaded the doors we'd be trapped in here just waiting for them to turn. By rights, as soon as we knew the apocalypse had begun we should have all stripped naked and examined each other thoroughly. So, don't think FAST in a zombie apocalypse. Always remember the FACTS.

THE FINAL GOODBYE (*The heading to this segment of the play might be displayed on an overhead projector or flip chart*)

DALE: So, that's it from us today. We hope you've learnt well with us. Of course, if there are any burning questions that you felt we haven't answered then we'll be around and about outside momentarily and we're happy to help. If you're rushing off we can also be contacted via our Facebook page called 'How To Survive A Zombie Apocalypse' or you could drop us a line on our message boards on our website at How To Survive A Zombie Apocalypse dot co dot uk or make sure you pick up the book Dr Dale's Zombie Dictionary, it has everything you'll need to know to thrive and survive when the undead revive. In the meantime, it's thank you from myself and the rest of the team and remember this one fact. The apocalypse is coming and we're your only hope of survival. Goodnight.

Dale, Judy and Donald exit

Tristen slowly gets up and realises that everyone has gone. He shuffles to the middle of the stage and smiles awkwardly at the audience and then starts to sing 'My Heart Will Go On'

Dale pokes his head back on stage

DALE: Tristen!!!

Tristen bows and leaves

THE END

How to Survive a Zombie Apocalypse RELOADED
by
Ben Muir

Characters

Although the 4 characters from the original show have been portrayed as both male or female, you may present the seminar in any gender mix you wish

If so, some aspects of the seminar script will need altering in order to present characters as alternate genders and should any lines need to be changed, please contact the author for approval (pronoun changes do not require approval).

The Original Characters were ...

Dr Dale Seslick
The Seminar leader. Cool, Calm, Collected, Charismatic. Fluent in zombie survival lore, he is never stumped for an answer. He punctuates his training seminars with continual use of hand gestures and buzz words.

Judy O'Dea
Dr Dale's second in command. She is scientific to a fault. Smart and to the point. She is the one who attempts to control the other two members of the team, although often gets drawn into the insanity unwillingly, she continues to act and react as if everything was carrying on normally.

Donald Straite
The aged survivalist who has followed every conspiracy theory in the book and has attempted and succeeded many difficult training exercises (he once lived for seven days up a flag pole with nothing to eat but a cheese sandwich). Very keen to be involved in all aspects of training but can get easily distracted if there is a pretty lady in the audience.

Tristen Granger
Dr Dale's nephew. He tries so, so hard but has absolutely no idea what is going on during the seminar. His stupidity is that of a childish wonderment - and he always tries to listen and understand what's going on... until his mind drifts and he starts thinking about puppies and clouds.

As the audience enters the auditorium, they are greeted by Donald, Judy and Tristen who supply each of them with a double sided card. Each card has 'A' printed on one side and 'B' printed on the other

Inside, the stage is set with a lectern centre and four chairs - two either side and slightly back from the lectern.

Around the walls of the auditorium, placed to look like theatre row allocations are 8 cards which say A1, B2, A3, B4, A5, B6, A7, B8 - these cards can be altered dependant on the shape of the room as long as the letter and numbers correspond to the correct answer to each numbered question.

Once the audience is in, the cast leaves and the lights dim. The opening track – opening intro music is available from Funcast Ltd - begins and Judy, Donald and Tristen re-enter at the specific points in the music that reference their area of expertise. They sit on the chairs - Donald Far SR, Judy Near SR, Tristen far SL.

At the end of the music Dr Dale enters, and stands behind the lectern.

DALE: Good evening and welcome to How To Survive a Zombie Apocalypse, I'm Dr Dale, author of Dr Dale's Zombie Dictionary and founder of the School of Survival or, as we like to call it, S.O.S (*hand gesture*) and I'm here to teach you today - How To Survive A Zombie Apocalypse. Now here at the School of Survival... or S.O.S. (*hand gesture*) we don't believe in just standing there and talking at you (*hand gesture*), expecting you to soak it all up like a sponge. No. That's not how we roll. (*hand gesture*) No - we believe in Inclusion with a capital I. (*hand gesture*) Working together as a team. Inviting you to participate. Invoking Team Work And Togetherness (hand gesture). We expect you to get involved with us. Share your thoughts, theories and ideas. In fact, to start you off slowly, let's just try a little bit of that inclusion now. Very simple question for you. I want to know, how many people here believe, as of this moment, that they could survive a zombie apocalypse.

Audience put hands up. Dr Dale reacts accordingly with surprise or disappointment.

DALE: Okay, well let's break this down shall we into separate levels of training. Just so we get an idea of how much we need to teach you. What kind of people are in here? Firstly, put your hand up if you really don't think you could survive at all. You're the kind of person that we might as well sacrifice for the good of all as soon as we hear the apocalypse has begun.

Audience put hands up. Dale reacts accordingly.

DALE: Okay, now who thinks they are at an intermediate level? You've got a good chance of survival. You've seen some zombie films, played zombie games, read zombie books. You've got a basic idea about the zombie mythology.

Audience puts hands up and Dale reacts

DALE: Okay, now who here believes they are a true expert? And by expert I mean you know what weapons you'd take, where you'd head to, which close family member you'd sacrifice if the need arose.

Audience puts hands up

DALE: Okay, that's good. I tell you what, just stand up for me if you believe that you are a true survivor.

Audience stands up

DALE: I want everyone to see the confidence that seeps from your pores. That's it! Everyone else, just take a look at these people. These are the people who are trained for survival, they think about how to react in the apocalypse every day and surely that should inspire the rest of you to pull your finger out and start learning how to survive because currently these are the people who will be left to build the human race! Is that what you want? These people! The future of civilisation?! No, I thought not, so that is why you're all here today to learn so that it won't be just these happy few repopulating together to rebuild humanity. Okay, thanks guys, sit yourselves down.

Audience sit down

DALE: Okay now we know a little bit about you. That we've got some experts and remedials I think maybe it's time I introduced you to some special people who will be working closely with me to work closely with you. You see no man works alone on such a great endeavour as learning how to survive. No, I work alone as a team, and I'd like to introduce you to that team now. First off, our survival expert Mr Donald Straite. Now Donald, do you have any survival tips that you'd like to share with the team?

Donald stands

DONALD: Oh yes! My tip would be to stock up on food and supplies now. Tins of pilchards, cheese, other food. You never know when the apocalypse is going to begin and you need to have supplies prepared so that you're not short.

Donald sits.

DALE: Thank you, Donald, wise words from a man who knows a lot about being short. Okay moving on, Judy, the science expert. Judy, do you have anything you'd like to share?

Judy stands

JUDY: Oh yes! Recently I've been experimenting with the effectiveness of cattle prods as a weapon and I have discovered that, at their highest setting, an industrial cattle prod can fry a brain beyond repair in 3.2 seconds.

Judy sits

DALE: Thank you, Judy. Trying out the effectiveness of weapons is indeed important. And finally Tristen, do you have anything to share with us?

Tristen stands

TRISTEN: Cattle prods hurt

Tristen sits

DALE: Okay, thank you, Tristen. Now, those of you who have taken part in our live seminar before will know that before we get the teaching rolling there is something very important that we have to get out of the way first, and that is teaching you what exactly you'll be up against. You see, there is the potential for many different kinds of zombie to rear their heads when the time comes, and if we were to focus on all the different forms in the live seminar then things might get slightly confusing. So, we chose to focus on one specific kind of zombie, a zombie that has four specific rules attached to it. And before we begin teaching you how to survive, we're going to teach you what you're surviving from. So this is the part that the avid learners amongst you might want to start making notes.

123 ZOMBIE *(The heading to this segment of the play might be displayed on an overhead projector or flip chart)*

Dale moves the lectern to FSL and Tristen, Judy and Donald each take a card from the lectern and hold them so the numbers aren't facing the audience. All the cards have numbers on. It is important that the numbers are large and in a calculator font. Tristen is first in line and has '1', Judy is second in line and has '2', Donald is third in line and has '0'

DALE: Okay, so the four rules that apply to the zombie we will be dealing with today are as follows. Rule number One.

Tristen turns his card

TRISTEN: A zombie is dead.

DALE: Rule number one

TRISTEN: A zombie is dead

DALE: Yes, a zombie is dead! In some forms of media such as 28 days later, 28 weeks later, Left 4 Dead, Zombies are portrayed as live human beings that have been infected by some form of virus that makes them crave human flesh or a little bit angry. These are not zombies. A live human being who wants to eat another live human being is called a cannibal and this is not 'How To Survive A Cannibal Apocalypse'- that's next year. So! Rule number one.

TRISTEN: A zombie is dead.

DALE: Good. So next up, it's to do with how the infection is passed on. So, rule number two is…

Judy turns her card

JUDY: The infection is passed on by biting

DALE: Quite simply, if you are bitten by a zombie you will end up dead and you will reanimate as a zombie. Okay, good. So moving on to the next rule. How do we destroy a zombie? Well, this is done in a very specific way and is explained in rule number three.

Donald turns his card

DONALD: There is NO cure.

DALE: Whoa, wait a minute Donald…

DONALD: There is no cure.

DALE: Donald, that's rule number four.

DONALD: Yes, but I've got O. Nooo Cure.

DALE: Yes, Donald I know that's the one you've got, but you're in position for rule number three.

DONALD: But I've got noooo cure.

DALE: But you can't do rule number four before doing rule number three.

DONALD: I haven't got any other rule.

TRISTEN: I could do rule number three!

DALE: Okay, well, do you have a number three card?

TRISTEN: No.

Dale passes him a number three card off the lectern.

DALE: Okay, well you do rule number three, then. You do know rule number three don't you?

TRISTEN: Yes.

Dale turns back to the audience and doesn't see Tristen move to the end of the line after Donald, so Judy is first.

DALE: Okay, team, sorry about this. Just a bit of a mix up there. We're going to start this again so as not to get confused. The four rules are as follows. Rule number one...

Nothing

DALE: Rule number one?

Nothing

DALE: Judy. Rule number one.

JUDY: I'm rule number two.

DALE: You're in position for Rule number one.

JUDY: Yes, but I'm rule number two.

DALE: I know that, but you're in position for rule....

JUDY: I'm number two.

DALE: Right, well, who's rule number one!

TRISTEN: I was doing rule number one, but you told me to do rule number three.

DALE: But you need to do rule number one.

TRISTEN: Oh!

DONALD: No, I'm O- noooo cure.

Tristen moves back into position one.

DALE: Right, sorry about this, guys, we'll start again. Rule number one.

TRISTEN: A zombie is dead

DALE: Rule number two

JUDY: The infection is passed on by biting

DALE: Rule number three.

DONALD: There is no cure.

DALE: Donald that's rule number four!

DONALD: Yes, but it's all I've got. Noooo Cure.

DALE: Tristen, I thought you were doing rule number three.

TRISTEN: You told me to do rule number one.

DALE: But I expected you to move and do rule number three after doing rule number one.

TRISTEN: Well you didn't explain that properly.

DALE: I tell you what, forget it, Judy, can you do rule number three?

Dale hands Judy another number three card. Judy goes to move.

JUDY: Of course.

DALE: Whoa! Don't move yet. Don't forget you've got to do rule number two first.

JUDY: Oh yes.

DALE: Okay, right, sorry about this, guys. We need to make sure this is right though, as we wouldn't want anyone getting confused at the importance of these rules. Okay, let's start again. Rule number one.

TRISTEN: A zombie is dead.

DALE: Rule number two

JUDY: The infection is passed on by biting.

Judy moves into position on the other side of Donald

DALE: Rule number three

DONALD: There is no cure.

DALE: Donald!

DONALD: What? It's all I've got! Can this not be rule number three?

DALE: You're not even in position for rule number three, Donald.

DONALD: I'm not?

DALE: No, you're in position for rule number two!

DONALD: Am I?

DALE: Yes.

DONALD: That's not right, is it? I think you must be getting mixed up Dr Dale.

DALE: Look! Can we just take a moment to get this sorted. Who is number two?

JUDY: I am.

DALE: Well you don't want to be stood there, do you Judy?

JUDY: No, sorry.

Judy moves back into the middle position for rule number two.

DALE: Right, so if you're number one, Tristen and you're number two Judy, who's number three?

TRISTEN: Well I'm number three!

Dale gives Tristen another number three card

DALE: Well move into position for number three.

TRISTEN: Okay.

Tristen moves into position three at the end of the line.

DALE: Okay, that's good, now who's doing number one?

JUDY: Well now I'm in position for number one.
DALE: Do you mind doing number one? As you're in that position.

JUDY: Well on this occasion I suppose I could.

Dale passes Judy another number one card

DALE: Just make sure you give Donald the number two card.

JUDY: Right.

Judy gives Donald her number two card.

DONALD: Okay.

DALE: Now is everybody sorted?

All: Yes.

DALE: The important thing is you just need to make sure you are in the correct position for the rule you are giving out. Okay?

All: Right.

DALE: So, sorry about this guys. I think we're finally ready to go through these rules, sorry about the delay, but getting the details right is important. So! Rule number one!

Tristen moves back to stand next to Judy in position two

TRISTEN/JUDY: A zombie is dead

DALE: Rule number two

Donald moves back in between Tristen and Judy

DONALD: The infection is passed on by biting.

DALE: Rule number three

Judy moves to stand in position three next to Tristen

TRISTEN/JUDY: You must destroy the brain

DALE: Rule number four

Donald moves to the end of the line into position three

DONALD: There is no cure.
DALE: excellent. Now those are the four rules that you need to remember as told to you by Donald, Tristen and Judy.

The three of them muster to get into that order.

DALE: The thing you have to remember is that if you put all those rules together as one. There's only one thing they add up to.

The team hold all their cards up and it spells 'ZOMBIE' as in the picture below.

THE ELIMINATOR PART 1 (*The heading to this segment of the play might be displayed on an overhead projector or flip chart*)

(*Donald exits*).

DALE: Okay, so now we know the rules of the zombie we'll be dealing with, it's time to get down to the nitty gritty of learning how to survive. But today, we're not just going to be teaching you how. We'll be seeing if you can. You see, according to the Mayan Calendar as written by...

JUDY: Simon Mayo

DALE: The world is going to end very soon, and we want to make sure that you are ready. You see come the apocalypse, we won't be there to hold your hands. We'll be locked down in the fully automated, electronically capable school of survival in an undisclosed location to keep people like you away from us and our masses of supplies and weapons. But we don't just want to leave you floundering out there. We need to know that you are ready. So this is why we have concocted this test to see if you are ready. The Eliminator!

Tristen hits a remote control and the theme music of Who Wants To Be A Millionaire plays.

Donald brings on the score board pictured below

DALE: Now, this test is very simple. You are all going to work as a team to see just how many points you can score. We're pitting you against other audiences who have seen the show to see just which team is the most ready to survive. The way you climb the board is simple. I ask you a series of multiple choice questions and you utilise your cards to tell me if the answer is A or B. If you get the question wrong you are eliminated from answering any further questions but, as a team the ones who got it right play on. The way you climb the board is on a majority rules vote. So, if a higher number of you pick A and it is the correct answer then those who chose B will be eliminated, but because more of you picked the right answer you will move up the board. If, however, the majority of you pick A and it is the wrong answer then not only will you get eliminated, you will also move down the board. All very simple.

TRISTEN: Hey! I'm less than normal.

DALE: Yes Tristen, yes you are.

DONALD: And I'm seventy.

JUDY: If we're being kind...

DALE: Now there are a few other points to bear in mind. Down here are smiley faces - they are bonus points. Each member of my team has the option to give away one batch of bonus points throughout the game if we think someone has acted in an exemplary survivalist manner. That could be a question you ask in the Q & A session or anything at all really. You may need those bonus points to hit the high score. Then there's these little fellows down here! What are they?

TRISTEN: They are zombies.

DALE: Yes, I know, but what do they do?

TRISTEN: Kill people.

DALE: Well, yes, if they were real they would, but what do they mean in the game? Well, we'll find that out later. So, the rules are pretty simple. You're working together with the rest of your team to score the highest possible score. So if we're ready, let's play - The Eliminator!

Nothing

DALE: Tristen. The Eliminator.

TRISTEN: Oh, sorry!

Tristen hits the remote and plays the intro

DALE: No, Tristen, you can't just play it now. You have to wait until I say Eliminator...

Tristen hits the remote and plays the intro

DALE: Tristen, I have to say eliminator....

Tristen hits the remote and plays the music

DALE: Give me that!

Dale snatches the remote off Tristen

TRISTEN: But you said eliminator!

DALE: Yes, but you have to wait until I do it in a dramatic fashion. Donald, can you do it.

DONALD: Oh yes.

Donald takes the remote but spots a woman in the audience and stares at her

DALE: Right, so. If we're ready to begin. Let's play The Eliminator!

Nothing

DALE: Donald!

DONALD: Sorry, I just spotted that lady there and thought she'd be excellent for when we have to repopulate the world.

DALE: Donald. Just play the music.

Donald hits the remote and Barry White starts to play, he slinks over sexily to the lady he was referring to.

DALE: Donald!

DONALD: Oh, sorry.

DALE: Turn it off!

Donald tries to turn it off but the music switches to a Mexican Mariachi band. Donald tries to stop it, but it won't work.

DALE: Judy!

Judy takes the remote from Donald and presses it. The music turns off. She fiddles with the remote.

JUDY: There we go, Dr Dale, I've configured it to voice recognition. It should be fine now.

DALE: Thank you. So, let's play. The Eliminator!

Intro Music - Judy takes the A card and Donald takes the B card from the lectern

DALE: Okay, so we're going to start you off at an average score of 30 to set you on the way. Couple of easy questions to begin with, just to get you warmed up. So, question one. Out of these two which would you say was the more effective weapon in a zombie apocalypse? is it A

JUDY: A machete?

DALE: Or B

DONALD: A sponge?

DALE: Is it A

JUDY: A Machete?

DALE: Or B

DONALD: A sponge?

DALE: Okay, all hold your cards up and vote now!

DALE: Yes, the correct answer was of course 'A machete'. Don't forget that anything at all can be used as a weapon in the apocalypse if you use well thought out methodology, but there's no need to go for the more obscure option if items like a machete are readily available to you. So, the majority voted correct so you're moving up the board!

Music plays

DALE: If you happen to have been eliminated then, to avoid cheating, can you throw your cards back onto the stage.

The audience generally throw their cards in a manner designed to hit the performers.

Tristen usually gives his bonus points for good manners if someone hands him their card.

DALE: Okay, good start, so let's move onto question number two. In the event of a zombie apocalypse which of these two locations is the safest place to be? Is it A

DONALD: A hospital?

DALE: Or B

JUDY: A castle... made of steel... on a hill... with a moat..... filled with sharks... and a force shield around it?

DALE: Is it A?

DONALD: A hospital

DALE: Or B?

JUDY: ...what I just said.

DALE: Okay, vote now!

Audience vote

DALE: Yes, the correct answer was a castle. With all the added mod cons that Judy listed. A hospital would be a terrible place to be, seeing as, on being injured and bitten, that is the first place that most stupid people would go. They would then die, reanimate and you would end up with a hospital filled with zombies. That said, there is actually one time when a hospital is the safest place to be in a zombie apocalypse and that is if you happen to be in a coma. We have researched this heavily and, according to the documentaries Walking Dead, Resident Evil and 28 days Later, you have a higher percentage chance of surviving a zombie apocalypse if you are in a coma in a hospital when it begins. The lesson learnt there, being, if you are in a coma at the beginning of a zombie apocalypse then immediately make your way to a hospital. However, that is only one circumstance where you would be safe, castle was obviously the correct answer so if you picked hospital you've been eliminated. The rest of you, well done. You're moving up the board!

Music plays

DALE: Okay. Question three. Getting a bit harder now. Is the zombie apocalypse A

JUDY: A challenge?

DALE: or B

DONALD: A disaster?

DALE: Is the apocalypse A

JUDY: A challenge?

DALE: Or B

DONALD: A disaster?

DALE: Okay, I'll give you a moment to think about this. But I need you to have your final answer in now. *(Dale picks on someone who has chosen disaster)* Okay, why have you chosen disaster?

Generally speaking the audience member will say that it's the end of the world, great loss of life etc.

DALE: Meh! The correct answer is, of course, a challenge. All those who put disaster then throw your cards in. It probably won't be much of a surprise for you anyway, you probably expected to lose because you're just so negative! Let's move you up/down the scoreboard

Music

DALE: Going through the apocalypse with a nay say negative answer is the wrong thing to do. You've got to look on the positive side! If all your friends and family die, you don't have to worry about remembering birthdays anymore. Look, I think what we obviously need to do at this point is just take a break from the game and make you all a lot more positive. Get you all into the spirit of surviving. Because it's only by staying positive that you'll get through those dark days. So guys, what say we do some positive affirmations?

POSITIVE AFFIRMATIONS *(The heading to this segment of the play might be displayed on an overhead projector or flip chart)*

Donald sits in a central position between two people in the auditorium. Judy sits on the end of a row on the left of the auditorium so that one person is on her left. Tristen sits on the end of a row on the right of the auditorium making sure one person is on his right, preferably a man.

DALE: Okay, right, first off let's just ask you a simple question. Do you think you'll be the highest scoring team that we'll ever have in this game today?

AUDIENCE: Yes

DALE: Oh, come on now, I've told you to think positive! Will you be the highest scoring team?

AUDIENCE: Yes!

DALE: Right, well let me hear you say it! Say I will win!

AUDIENCE: I will win!

DALE: Excellent! That's more like it. But positive affirmations aren't just something that you would do to yourself. No. In a zombie apocalypse as we're learning here today, teamwork is important, and you need to share those positive affirmations with the rest of the team to help squash self-doubt. So, I want you to turn to the person on your left and say 'You will win!'

AUDIENCE: You will win

DALE: And now turn to the person on your right and say 'You will win!'

AUDIENCE: You will win!

DALE: Okay, does that make you feel better? Does that make you feel more like winners? Well, let's just try a few more to see if we can make you feel even more positive. Er... Judy - do you have any positive affirmations that you use?

JUDY: I am beautiful.

DALE: Which you are, so it must work. Okay, everybody try that then. Say 'I am beautiful.'

AUDIENCE: I am beautiful

DALE: Now turn to the person on your right and say 'You are beautiful'

AUDIENCE: You are beautiful

DALE: now turn to the person on your left and say 'You are beautiful'

AUDIENCE: You are beautiful

DONALD: Er! Dr Dale! Dr Dale!

DALE: Yes, Donald.

DONALD: It's just, well, I'm saying that this person on my left is beautiful... and well, they're not really.

DALE: Oh.

DONALD: I don't feel right saying it to them.

DALE: Erm... well how would you describe them?

DONALD: Moderately Okay.

DALE: Right, well, that's okay. We'll just change it then.

DONALD: Oh, right.

DALE: Just turn to the person on your left and say 'you are moderately okay'

AUDIENCE: You are moderately Okay

DONALD: Er Dr Dale!

DALE: Yes Donald?

DONALD: This person on my right just said I was moderately okay, and I called them beautiful!

DALE: Well, Donald, sometimes that's what happens. You know. You have to get used to these kind of mean spirited people in an apocalypse.

DONALD: It's just quite upsetting.

DALE: Just remember Donald, you are beautiful.

JUDY: No matter what they say.

TRISTEN: Words can't bring you down.

DALE: Okay, everybody happy?

JUDY: Er... actually, Dr Dale….

DALE: Yes Judy?

JUDY: I'm not particularly happy. You see, I'm turning to this person on my left and saying they're moderately okay but actually I think they're quite attractive and I wouldn't want them to think I'm being mean.

DALE: Well to be honest, they are quite attractive... erm... but I'm not sure...

TRISTEN: Dr Dale!

DALE: Yes Tristen?

TRISTEN: The person who is sat on my right who I'm calling beautiful…. Well, they're not. So maybe they could swap with Judy's friend.

DALE: Okay. That sounds like a good idea. *(Dale gets the names of the two people who are swapping for the sake of the script we will assume that the person who is sat next to Tristen is called Clive)* Okay, if you don't mind swapping than that would be great we just need to keep the positive vibes balanced in the room.

Clive and the person sat next to Judy swap places

DALE: Okay, right. Good, well, let's take the focus off physical attributes for the moment shall we, because it's not just about how you look... Er Tristen... what's your positive affirmation?

TRISTEN: I like Blue.

DALE: The colour or the boy band?

TRISTEN: The colour.

DALE: And do you like blue?

TRISTEN: Yes.

DALE: Well, it obviously works. But maybe it's not quite right for our affirmations today. Why don't we do I am Intelligent?

TRISTEN: I don't do that.

DALE: No. Right. Everybody say 'I am intelligent'

ALL: I am intelligent.

DALE: Now turn to the person on your left and say you are intelligent.

ALL: You are intelligent.

DALE: Now turn to the person on your right and say you are sublimely intelligent and intrinsically adept.

ALL: You are sublimely intelligent and intrinsically adept.

JUDY: Er! Dr Dale, I have a problem.

DALE: Yes Judy?

JUDY: Well, Clive just said that he's intelligent and clearly he's not.

DALE: Why?

JUDY: Well, he couldn't even manage to say it, so I'm not sure how he can be it.

DALE: Right... er....

JUDY: To be honest, I don't really want to be sat next to them in case some of it rubs off on me. You can catch stupidity y'know.

DALE: Okay, that's fine. I've got an idea. Donald wasn't happy with that person on his right calling him moderately okay, so why don't those two swap?

JUDY: Oh yes.

The person on Judy's left, and the person on Donald's right swap places.

TRISTEN: Er... Dr Dale, but now Donald will be calling Clive beautiful.

DALE: Oh yes.

DONALD: Well he can swap places with the person on my left.

DALE: Yes, but you said that they were only moderately okay.

DONALD: Yeah, but compared to Clive, they're beautiful.

The person on Donald's left swaps places with Clive.

DALE: Okay, right, sorry about this everyone, just need to make sure the positivity in the room is balanced. Right, but I think we've all got the right idea about it now. Maybe we could finish with something all encompassing. Repeat after me. I am beautiful

AUDIENCE: I am beautiful.

DALE: I am intelligent.

AUDIENCE: I am intelligent.

DALE: And I am a good person.

AUDIENCE: And I am a good person.

Judy stands up

JUDY: Dr Dale! I am not happy!

DALE: What?

JUDY: Clive just looked me straight in the eyes and said he was beautiful, intelligent and he was a good person. Now first off he's a bit of an ugo, secondly he's clearly thick and thirdly how can he be a good person if he's lying about those things straight to my face.

DALE: Now, Judy, calm down.

JUDY: Oh, it makes me so angry! People like that shouldn't be able to get away with it!

TRISTEN: Dr Dale! When I was naughty my mum used to make me stand in the corner.

DALE: Would that make you feel better Judy, if we made Clive stand in the corner?

JUDY: Yes, I think it would.

DALE: Right, Clive, could you go and stand in the corner.

Dale makes Clive stand in the back corner of the stage.

TRISTEN: Face the wall.

DALE: Yep, that's it.

JUDY: I'm sorry Dr Dale, it's just people like that they make me so angry.

DALE: No, that's fine Judy, it helps prove a point. You see there's always going to be people like that, apocalypse or not, but once you've removed the bad apples, what have you got? Apple sauce. And I think it helps in our positive affirmation exercise. Let's all just do one last affirmation together. Repeat after me - I will win.

AUDIENCE: I will win.

DALE: I am beautiful

AUDIENCE: I am beautiful.

DALE: I am intelligent.

AUDIENCE: I am intelligent.

DALE: And thank god I'm not Clive.

AUDIENCE: And thank god I'm not Clive.

DALE: Does that make you feel good?

AUDIENCE: Yeah!

DALE: Does that make you feel like winners!

AUDIENCE: Yeah!

DALE: Are you ready to be the top scoring team?

AUDIENCE: Yeah!

DALE: Okay then, let's play on!

ELIMINATOR PART TWO (*The heading to this segment of the play might be displayed on an overhead projector or flip chart*)

DALE: Okay, while we've still got the adrenaline pumping let's move on to question four.

Tristen takes card A, Judy takes card B.

DALE: If at the start of the apocalypse you end up with someone on your team who is potentially not beautiful, not intelligent and who might possibly be called Clive what should you do? Should you A ...

TRISTEN: Kill them?

DALE: or B ...

JUDY: Keep them around?

DALE: That's A ...

TRISTEN: Kill them.

DALE: Or B ...

JUDY: Keep them around.

The audience vote. At this point it's worth taking note of the people Clive actually came to the show with to see if they kill him or not and bonus points can be given out for how willing they are to kill him.

DALE: Okay, well, I can tell you that the correct answer was keep them around! In a zombie apocalypse, especially at the initial outbreak, it is always useful to have someone around who you don't mind sacrificing to either facilitate your own survival or escape or to eat should you run out of food. The Clives of the world are perfect candidates for that. So Clive, you're spared, you can sit back down. In fact, anyone who did move, if you want to make your way back to your original seat that's okay. Of course, If you prefer the person we've sat you next to you can stay exactly where you are.

Audience moves if they so wish

DALE: Okay you got that right/ wrong, those who chose Kill him throw your cards in and let's move you up/down the board

Music

DALE: Right. Question number five.

Alarm rings

DALE: Uh oh! What's that? Well, it means that these guys come into play ... (*reveals zombie stickers*)

Dr Dale slaps a zombie sticker on the arrow that marks the score

DALE: What does it mean? Well it means we play this question exactly as before. if you get it right you stay in the game and you move up one more step on the ladder, but if you get it wrong you not only get eliminated but you drop all the way back down to thirty points again. So, you need to concentrate really hard and make sure you're correct. Otherwise it could scupper your chances of being the highest scoring team. So, are you ready? Feeling positive? Then let's play question number five.

Music

DALE: Question number five. Out of these two - which is the better animal to have with you in a zombie apocalypse? Is it A

TRISTEN: A Giraffe?

DALE: Or B...

JUDY: A gorilla?

DALE: Is it A...

TRISTEN: A Giraffe?

DALE: Or B ...

JUDY: A gorilla?

DALE: Okay, I need you to make your final decision.

It's often wise to help them try and get it right as if they get it wrong the mood of the audience changes to one of negativity!

DALE: Well, I can tell you that the correct answer was A - a giraffe! *(congratulations or commiserations as they move up or down the board)*

Music

DALE: There is a reason for this. Giraffes are better because they are a much easier mode of transport to operate and can reach running speeds of up to 55 miles per hour. They also have very long necks which means you can use them to access or escape second storey buildings. They have a kick that can shatter a lion's skull which means that they are capable of both attack and defence. They also have extremely high blood pressure which means should animals be able to be infected they will have a potentially higher natural immunity and the change will happen at a slower pace. Gorillas are a bad choice because they are currently on the endangered species list whereas giraffes are not, so it must be pretty easy to get hold of a giraffe and should you lose the first one it would be easy to find another. They are notoriously difficult to communicate with unless you happen to be Sigourney Weaver and they are also the closest genetic match to human beings which means if any animal is likely to succumb to the zombie virus it will be gorillas and the last thing you want to be faced with is a zombie gorilla as they're just as bad as zombie clowns or zombie midgets. Okay! So, there we are. If you got it wrong throw your cards in. How many of you are still in the game? That's good! Remember, in this game it's quality not quantity that counts. As long as the intelligent ones are answering the questions you should do okay. But after that tense moment I think it might be time to have a breather and do the Question and Answer session.

QUESTION AND ANSWER SESSION *(The heading to this segment of the play might be displayed on an overhead projector or flip chart)*

In an hour long show there is usually time for three or four questions

ELIMINATOR PART THREE *(The heading to this segment of the play might be displayed on an overhead projector or flip chart)*

DALE: Okay, well that's about all the questions we can answer today, if you do have any more questions that we couldn't get round to we are going to be around after the show so we'll attempt to answer them then. But for now, let's play on with the eliminator!

Music

DALE: Right, let's just recap - you're on () points and how many of you are left playing? That's good. You're doing well. So, let's restart the game with a relatively simple question as we move onto question six.

Music

Donald takes card A, Judy takes card B.

DALE: Is fire a good weapon to use in a zombie apocalypse? A

DONALD: Yes.

DALE: B …

JUDY: No.

DALE: A…

DONALD: Yes.

DALE: B…

JUDY: No.

DALE: Simple question so vote now.

Audience vote

DALE: Well, I can tell you that the right answer is B - No! Fire is not a good weapon to use. So if you got it wrong, throw your cards in and let's move you up/down the board.

Music

DALE: I think the easiest way to explain the use of fire is through a quick simulation. We'll imagine for a moment that me and Judy are in my office at the school of survival enjoying a brandy and smoking a cigar. Donald if you could play the zombie.

DONALD: Oh yes.

TRISTEN: Can I have a part?

DALE: Er….. well…. You know I'd never usually invite you to join me in brandy and cigars…. I tell you what! You know that rug I've got.

TRISTEN: The bear rug?

DALE: Yes! If you could be that…

TRISTEN: Okay.

Tristen lies across the stage as a bear skin rug (with the growling head)

DALE: So, here's me and Judy enjoying our brandy and cigars when in comes a zombie! We throw the brandy then we throw the cigars and the zombie ignites. Problem is, as we know from rule number three, we must destroy the brain and fire won't do that immediately. We also know that zombies won't feel pain as all their nerve endings are dead. So, what you end up with is a flailing ball of fire that sets fire to the curtains, to Judy, to the whole room, even the rug….

Donald flails setting fire to Judy who begins to mime being on fire like the girl from the beginning of Tales of the Unexpected. Donald mounts Tristen and flails on top of him.

DALE: So, as you can see, fire was not a very good choice at all. It's completely ruined my entire office and all my associates.

TRISTEN: I'm ruined Dr Dale.

DALE: Thank you.

Tristen, Judy and Donald break from the simulation

DALE: Some people may think it's fine to use fire as a long range weapon, the problem, though, is it's difficult to control so you could fire a burning arrow into a building several miles away but the resulting fire could spread to your own safe house or cause structural damage to buildings you scavenge from so we recommend never to use fire if there is another more sensible alternative. Okay, let's keep on the subject of weapons as we move onto question seven. Now this one is based on a bit of a simulation so pay attention to the scenario and then chose the best course of action. Imagine you are in the middle of a zombie apocalypse and you have absolutely no weapon. Then you come across another survivor and they have a weapon. How are you going to get that weapon from them? Are you going to B…

DONALD: Attack?

DALE: Or A…

JUDY: Negotiate?

DALE: So is it B...

DONALD: Attack.

DALE: Or A...

JUDY: Negotiate.

DALE: So, which one is it? Raise your cards now. Okay - well I can tell you that the correct answer was....

JUDY: A - Negotiate.

DALE: The clue was in the question. They have a weapon, you don't. Why on earth would you attack them? So, if you got it wrong, throw in your cards, but the majority of you got it right / wrong so let's move you up/ down that board.

Music

R.A.P. (*The heading to this segment of the play might be displayed on an overhead projector or flip chart*)

DALE: Now, in a zombie apocalypse negotiation skills are going to be important. There are going to be other survivors and they are not going to want to give you their all important supplies. You won't want to risk an all-out war between survivors because ultimately that will reduce our chances of surviving the zombie apocalypse if the humans are fighting amongst themselves. This is why you need to learn negotiation skills. Now here at the school of survival we have come up with three distinctive and proven negotiation tactics that are guaranteed to get you what you want from who you want and these techniques are called RAP.

Judy, Donald and Tristen, snap in and out of a Gangsta pose whenever Dale says 'RAP'

DALE: But we don't mean RAP in the conventional sense of talking in rhyme over a juicy beat. No, we mean RAP as an acronym. It means Resistance, Assistance, Persistence. Or RAP. Now you may wonder what's so special about these techniques, well, I think we've got time to go through them and just show you so that you can learn them and take them away with you to use at a future date as you never know when you'll need to utilise skills such as these. So, why don't we set up a bit of a simulation? Er.... Judy, let's have you being the owner of some sort of weapons emporium. Donald I want you to come into the emporium and get an axe off Judy.

JUDY/DONALD: Okay

DALE: But before we go into RAP, what I want you to do is show what would happen if you were to use none of our patented guaranteed to work negotiation techniques.

JUDY/DONALD: Okay.

During the simulation everything is mimed and the mime axe is passed backwards and forwards as needed

DALE: So, here we go. The first simulation is Tristen outside about to be attacked by a zombie, Donald needs to get the axe to save him, so here's Donald trying to get an axe from Judy but without using RAP.
Donald mimes walking into the shop and up to Judy who is stood behind her counter. The mime axe is obviously on the wall behind her.

DONALD: Hello, I'd like that axe, please.

JUDY: No.

DONALD: Oh.
Donald leaves the shop and Tristen dies

DALE: So, there you have it. Despite Donald's best efforts he was unable to get the axe off Judy and Tristen dies,

Donald shrugs.

DALE: Now let's try this again, but this time using the first of our techniques – Resistance. So, Donald, go get that axe and save Tristen's life.

Donald mimes - opening the door and walks up to the counter.

DONALD: Hello I'd like that axe, please.

JUDY: No.

DONALD: Oh, that's okay I didn't want it anyway.

JUDY: Why not?

DONALD: The handle's too short.

JUDY: No it's not.

DONALD: The blade's the wrong shape.

JUDY: No it's not

DONALD: It's the wrong colour.

JUDY: No it's not. Take a look.

DONALD: Oh, nice axe.

JUDY: You can have it if you want.

DONALD: Thanks.

Donald takes the axe, exits the shop and saves Tristen.

DALE: So there we see that Donald has managed to get the axe and save Tristen.

Tristen hugs Donald.

DALE: That was resistance. Making Judy think he didn't want the axe made her give him the axe. That simple. Okay let's move onto the second one - Assistance!

TRISTEN: Dr Dale?

DALE: Yes.
TRISTEN: Can I have a go please?

DALE: Do you know how to do assistance?

TRISTEN: No.

DALE: Well which one do you know?

TRISTEN: Resistance.

DALE: Is that because you just saw Donald doing it.

TRISTEN: Yes.

DALE: Okay, well, I suppose there's no harm in doing Resistance again. It will give the team another chance to see it if they didn't pick up on the technique the first time. Okay guys, we're going to do resistance again. This time Donald is being attacked and Tristen is going to get the axe off Judy to save him.

Tristen mimes opening the door and approaches Judy.

TRISTEN: I'd like that axe, please.

JUDY: No.

TRISTEN: That's fine, I didn't want it anyway.

JUDY: Why not?

TRISTEN: The handle's too short.

JUDY: No it's not.

TRISTEN: The blade's the wrong shape.

JUDY: No it's not.

TRISTEN: It's the wrong colour.

JUDY: No it's not, here have a look.

TRISTEN: Oh, nice axe.

JUDY: You can have it if you want, I didn't want it anyway.

TRISTEN: Why not?

JUDY: The handles too short, the blade's the wrong shape and it's the wrong colour.

TRISTEN: No it's not. Here have a look.

JUDY: Oh, nice axe.

TRISTEN: You can have it if you want.

JUDY: Thanks

Tristen leaves the shop happy.

DALE: No, Tristen! Tristen!

TRISTEN: What?

DALE: What're you doing?

TRISTEN: Getting the axe.

DALE: Well, where is it?

TRISTEN: I gave it back.

DALE: But what's happening to Donald?

Donald is dying slowly.

TRISTEN: He's melting?

DALE: No! He's being killed by a zombie! The point of the exercise is not to give the axe away. Okay? Donald!

DONALD: Yes.

DALE: Can you show him again?

DONALD: Oh yes.

TRISTEN: Should I be being attacked?

DALE: No just watch.

Donald enters the shop and approaches Judy.

DONALD: Can I have that axe please.

JUDY: No.
DONALD: Oh, I didn't really want it anyway.

JUDY: Good 'cos you're not having it.

DONALD: Er….. but I want it!

JUDY: You're not having it.

DALE: Judy! What are you doing?

JUDY: Keeping the axe.

DALE: Why?

JUDY: You said the point of the exercise was not to give the axe away.

DALE: No, I was talking to Tristen. Tristen isn't supposed to give the axe away. The point of the exercise is to give the axe away!

JUDY: Why would I do that?

DALE: Because the axe is flawed. There's a problem with the axe.

JUDY: Ah! Right! Okay.

DALE: Right, let's try it again.

Donald exits the shop and re-enters and approaches Judy.

JUDY: Here! Take this axe!

DONALD: I don't want it, you have it!

JUDY: I don't want it!

DONALD: Take the axe!

DALE: What are you doing?

JUDY: Giving the axe away! You said!

DALE: Donald? Why don't you take it?

DONALD: You said it was a flawed axe. I'm not fighting zombies with a flawed axe.

DALE: No, Judy thinks it's flawed!

DONALD: She's the shop keeper. She must be an expert. If she thinks it's flawed then it's flawed.

DALE: There is nothing wrong with this axe! Tristen! Look at it!

TRISTEN: It doesn't look right to me.

DALE: Right! Fine! Forget the axe!

Dale throws the mime axe on the floor.

DALE: We'll pick another weapon.

TRISTEN: Oh! Oh! A lightsaber (*mimes light saber*) A tommy gun!! (*mimes tommy gun*) Oh! A lion (*does rubbish lion impression*)

DALE: No, how about something more sensible like a broadsword.

DONALD: Oh yes! A broadsword! I could be a knight in shining armour riding across the fields looking for my damsel in distress.

Donald mimes riding a horse slowly and majestically. It looks marginally like slow grinding.

DALE: Donald. No. You can't be a knight.

DONALD: Oh, why.

DALE: Because a knight would already have a broadsword, wouldn't he. You would have to be someone without a broadsword.

DONALD: Hmmm. Yes. Someone without a broadsword. (*thinks for a moment and then starts skipping around the stage like a demented pixie*) Aaahhhh top o' d morning to ya! A begorah!

DALE: DONALD: What are you doing?

DONALD: I'm being a leprechaun. They wouldn't have a broadsword.

DALE: Look, why don't you be someone more sensible? Copy someone from the audience. Who here doesn't have a broadsword?

Show of hands

DALE: Okay, a lot of people own broadswords. That's worrying (*points at someone in the front row who doesn't have a broadsword*) Okay, be him.

Tristen runs up to the person who Dale picked

TRISTEN: Okay, I'd like a trip to Disney World, a bar of fruit and nut and a puppy called Puppy.

DALE: What are you doing?

TRISTEN: Making my wishes.

DALE: What?

TRISTEN: Well he doesn't have a broadsword, so he must be a leprechaun.
DALE: No! It doesn't work like that! He's not a leprechaun!

TRISTEN: He's not?

DALE: No!

TRISTEN: This is just like the time Judy said Santa Claus was dead.

DALE: Judy?

JUDY: I didn't say he was dead. I said that he must have supernatural powers in order to get around the world in one night so he must be a vampire and therefore undead.

DALE: Okay, see, that's different. Right, forget the broadsword. Let's try a katana.

JUDY: Banana?

DALE: Katana.

JUDY: Banana?

DALE: Katana!

JUDY: Banana?

DALE: Banana!

JUDY: That's a stupid weapon.

DALE: Look, there are no axes, no light sabers, no tommy guns, no lions, no broadswords, no katanas…

JUDY: And no bananas?

DALE: Yes! You have no bananas.

JUDY: We have no bananas today.

TRISTEN: Oh well, this is a rubbish weapons shop!

DONALD: I don't know why we came here in the first place!

TRISTEN: They've nothing in.

DONALD: We might as well go somewhere else.

DALE: Look, no wait! I'll buy the shop.

JUDY: Hey! What about my mortgage?

DALE: I have paid off the mortgage.

JUDY: Oh good! And my dogs?

DALE: No, you can take your dogs.

Judy walks imaginary dogs from behind the counter and they leave the shop. Dale takes up the position behind the counter

DALE: Right! I have completely restocked the shop. Tristen, come and try and get a weapon from me.

DONALD: Oh! Can I not do it, Dr Dale?

DALE: No Donald, you messed it up twice in a row. It's Tristen's turn now.

DONALD: Oh, but Dr Dale!

DALE: No, Donald, go and stand over there and watch.

Donald moves across the stage and trips over where the imaginary axe on the floor was dropped by Dale.

DONALD: Ow!!!!

DALE: What is it now?

DONALD: I just tripped over that axe that you left on the floor.

DALE: What?

JUDY: Oh no, Dr Dale! He fell over the axe! He's hurt himself!

DONALD: It really hurts.

DALE: This is ridiculous.

JUDY: Ridiculous? Really? Now you're mocking him. Well, we'll see just how mocking you are when we take you to court. It was clearly your fault and Donald might not be able to walk again. You could have to pay millions in compensation.

DALE: But that's not the truth.

JUDY: You can't handle the truth!

DALE: Judy?

JUDY: I'm off to get my camera so I can take some pictures of that axe for evidence to show how negligent you are. Come on, Donald.

Judy helps Donald limp off.

DALE: Tristen!

TRISTEN: Yes?

DALE: I need you to get rid of that axe.

TRISTEN: What? Why?

DALE: Don't ask questions. Just get it out of here before Judy gets back to take pictures of it.

TRISTEN: Where should I take it?

DALE: Anywhere! Just get rid of it! It's there on the floor!

TRISTEN: I can see it!

Tristen picks up the axe and exits.

Dale is quite flustered. He turns his back to the audience to think...

DALE: Now where was I....?

Tristen pokes his head back on stage.

TRISTEN: Guys! I got the axe!

Donald and Judy step back on the other side of the stage and give a cheesy thumbs up.

Dale spins back round to face the audience - he is back to his charming self.

DALE: And that is how to get the axe using Assistance. The three of them worked together to confound and confuse the shopkeeper into giving over the axe. Okay, so that's resistance and assistance, just one final negotiation technique to show you and we're done. But for that we'll need to set everything back up again. Tristen can I have the axe?

TRISTEN: No.

DALE: Tristen. Gimme the axe.

TRISTEN: No

DALE: Tristen. Gimme the axe.

TRISTEN: No

This continues for absolutely ages. It needs to go on with a couple of pauses where Dale stops to consider other things to say but just carries on saying 'Gimme the Axe' Tristen also needs to start cutting Dale off in one of the segments. Basically, you want the audience to feel uncomfortable because it's gone on so long and then start laughing again because it's gone past the uncomfortable stage. The last 10 times of the repeat need to be done at super speed.

DALE: Gimme the axe.

TRISTEN: No.

DALE: Tristen. Gimme the axe.

TRISTEN: No.

DALE: Gimme the axe.

TRISTEN: No.

DALE: Tristen. Gimme the axe.

TRISTEN: Okay.

Tristen gives Dale the axe.

DALE: And that is persistence! Okay, so there you have it, Resistance, Assistance, Persistence. The three ways you'll be able to negotiate getting anything you want in a zombie apocalypse. Or as we prefer to call them - RAP.

THE ELIMINATOR PART FOUR *(The heading to this segment of the play might be displayed on an overhead projector or flip chart)*

DALE: Okay, so now you can all walk away knowing that you've learnt something practical, it's time to move on with our next question in the eliminator.

Alarm sounds

DALE: Oh no! Another danger question! So close to the end as well. I think that you're all feeling positive, though, aren't you? Good. Because this is the last question and if you get this wrong you will drop back down to thirty again, which would be such a shame at this stage as you've done so well so far. But let's not get despondent! Let's keep positive as we go into question eight!

Music

Tristen picks up card B, Judy picks up card A

DALE: In a zombie apocalypse - what is the best form of attire? Is it A...

JUDY: Rubber?

DALE: Or B...

TRISTEN: Skin Tight Lycra?

DALE: Is it A...

JUDY: Rubber?

DALE: Or B...

TRISTEN: Skin Tight Lycra?

DALE: Okay I need you to think about this carefully. I really, really don't want you to get this wrong.

Once the decision has been made, Dale can ask the rest of the audience if they think that the right answer has been chosen. He can even ask them if they want to change their minds. Again, it's quite all right to lead the audience into getting it right as it makes them leave with a feel-good feeling if they do well!

DALE: Okay, is that your final answer? Well I can tell you that the correct answer was............ A - Rubber. Who would want a car that had tyres made of lycra? It would be completely useless. Best tyres are rubber tyres. So, if you got it wrong throw your cards in, if you got it right well done. We'll move you up/down the board. What we also do is count how many people still hold their cards and we add that to your final score and along with your bonus points you have so far scored (). Give yourselves a round of applause.

Applause

DALE: It doesn't end there though, because I am going to give you the chance to double your points. Not only that but I will uneliminate everyone in the room which means you'll also get to add an extra () points onto your final score too. But there's a catch. To do this you have to gamble. One final question. If you get it right then your score is doubled and you all get uneliminated. If you get it wrong, you drop down to zero points. That means you'll be left with your bonus points and survivor points only, which is a very very low score. So, what do you want to do? Gamble or stick?

The audience have never not gambled. But you might want to prepare a contingency should they not.

DALE: Okay! You're going to gamble! That's what we like to see! Thinking positive! You can do it! So, I'm going to ask one more question and if that question is answered correctly then you will double your points and all of you will be uneliminated. And that one, final question is going to be asked to...... Clive!

Audience usually react with major disappointment

DALE: Hey! Come on! Let's give him some support! Positive affirmations!

Audience shout positive affirmations at Clive.

DALE: Good! That's it! Have faith. Now the rest of you need to keep quiet as, if there is cheating and anyone tells him the answer, you will automatically be disqualified and you will lose the gamble. So, let's let him concentrate. Now Clive, I'm not an unfair man. I'm going to give you three chances to answer this question correctly. Okay, are you ready?

Clive: Yes.

DALE: Without having seen this show before, there is a guaranteed way that everyone in this room should have got every single question correct and thus all of you would have remained uneliminated. What was it?

Remember - it is a 'guaranteed way' so if he answers read the book, there is no guaranteed way anyone could retain all the information in the book.

After two incorrect answers Dale can offer...

DALE: Okay Clive, I tell you what, you've only got one try left. I'm going to give you the option to phone a friend. You can pass this answer over to anyone else. If there's someone else in this room who you think might know the answer I'm going to let you pass your final try over to them.
Clive will either pick someone else to answer for him or he will answer himself.

React accordingly to whether it is the correct answer or not.

DALE: The answer was that the answers to all the questions have been written on the walls the entire night. Those signs aren't row or seat allocations, they are the answers to the questions. A was the answer to one; A was the answer to two; B was the answer to three and so on. The one person who should have seen that was the only person who has been sat in three different locations and viewpoints around the room. That being Clive!

Tristen turns the score board round on which will be written the scores of all the other teams. He calls tonight's team Clive's Team

DALE: So, your final score was ()

Dale and the team can comment on how well they've done in comparison to other teams etc.

DALE: But that's it from us. I think we can safely say that when the apocalypse comes and we at the school of survival lock ourselves in our fully automated zombie proof stronghold that today we have learnt that you will all survive (die) without us. Of course, in the meantime, before it all begins we recommend you continue your training, and if you need any help, we can be contacted via Facebook on our page - How To Survive A Zombie Apocalypse , at our website - 'How To Survive A Zombie Apocalypse dot co dot uk and we must recommend you buy the book Dr Dale's Zombie Dictionary as it has everything you've learnt tonight in it and much much more but for now….

The Zombie Alarm sounds.

DALE: Judy, what's it doing? The game's over!

Judy turns the alarm off and checks the remote

JUDY: I don't know. Hang on, let me check…. Oh!

DALE: Oh?

JUDY: It's not part of the game. It's the actual alarm! The apocalypse has begun!

Donald and Tristen move in to listen.

DALE: Oh right! Okay, well, I think we're in pretty safe hands here, we all know what to do when the zombies…

JUDY: Dr Dale…

DALE: What?

JUDY: It's not zombies.

DALE: What?

JUDY: It's robots.

DALE: What does it say?

The intro to Battlestar Galactica plays…

JUDY: It says.... They were created by man.... They rebelled.... They evolved.... There are many copies.... And they have a plan.

Music ends.

DALE: So you mean to say that we've spent all our time researching a zombie apocalypse and it's robots...?

JUDY: Yes.

DALE: Well, I feel rather foolish.

JUDY: What shall we do?

DALE: Okay, it's fine, it's fine, just follow my lead.

The Terminator theme sting begins

Tristen, Judy and Donald pose behind Dr Dale

DALE: Hi, I'm Dr Dale and I'm here today to teach you how to survive a robot apocalypse. We've got all the skills you'll need to see you through those dark days ahead. So, come with us if you want to live!

Music reaches its crescendo.

Blackout.